MW01145283

# OVERWHELMED

### A MOTHER'S STORY OF INSPIRATION...IT WILL MAKE YOU CRY, IT WILL MAKE YOU THINK, IT WILL CHANGE YOUR LIFE FOREVER.

## RITA B. DAVIS

Outskirts Press, Inc.
Denver, Colorado

Outskirts Press, Inc.
http://www.outskirtspress.com

ISBN: 978-1-4327-1110-8

Outskirts Press and the "OP" logo are trademarks belonging to Outskirts Press, Inc.

PRINTED IN THE UNITED STATES OF AMERICA

IN LOVING MEMORY OF

JOHN C. "CHAUNCE" DAVIS

# Reflection

*WHAT I HAVE LEARNED AND HOW I HAVE GROWN FROM THIS LIFE EXPERIENCE*

# About the Author

My life as a child was a very challenging one, including my insecurities, and low self-esteem. I recall feeling very disappointed about not being able to fit in with children in my class, my environment as a whole. I was raised within a large family, with 9 children, myself being the youngest. I did not have a normal or average childhood. My mother was able to raise nine (9) children with only a yearly salary of less than $3,000.00 per year. I recall having to complete college financial aid application forms, and being asked to enter my mother's yearly salary. I was even shocked myself to realize she earned so little, but was able to give us, our family, so much. We did have a father in our lives. We would sit down to dinner and he would say the prayer. He worked hard to provide for nine children. We had a family who understood and believed in family values. However, one day he had to begin working out of town and he would send money to mom to take care of household bills, food, clothing, and other expenses for nine (9) children, as well as, herself. It seemed that he expected her to work a miracle in getting the small amounts of money he sent, every two weeks, to cover such a multitude of expenses. He would only send $25.00-$50.00 to mom. But you know, I don't remember ever starving or going without. Mom always had a way of making things come together. I remember how we always made a few groceries every week, mostly on Saturday evenings. There was a store on the street over from where we lived, and they allowed mom to get food and other items on credit. The Lord always had a way of working things out for the good. Whenever school started, or an event was coming up, in which we needed money for various reasons, mom had a way of going downtown on the city bus, we assumed to the bank, and because of her good credit she always maintained, she was able to borrow the money she needed. Mom believed in saving what money she could, and always paying back any money she had to borrow. I have memories of my mother going to work, morning after morning, dressed in her pure white uniform dress, as she walked down the street and through a pathway to the next street. This she would do in the sun, rain, sleet, and yes, even the snow!! She worked as a dedicated cafeteria staff worker, both as a cook, and cashier. She worked in that one school for more than twenty-six (26) years.

As I look back over those years of my life, and our childhood, I realized that God had plans for mom and ordered her steps as he has done in my life. I know now that if it had not been for mom working in that cafeteria, we may not have had enough to eat. She was able to bring home leftovers from that cafeteria, which really helped to feed our family. I recalled eating those good brownies, fish cakes, and rice crispy bars. Mom also never forgot us on those days they had Thanksgiving and Christmas dinners, those were meals to remember, when the old way of cooking existed. She and the other cafeteria ladies, knew how to put together a scrumptious dinner you could truly enjoy. I remember how those ladies treated us like family, and loved us like we were their own. In those days, those cafeteria ladies knew what it meant to COOK!! I mean really COOK!! I soon began to realize what God means, when he says, "I won't put any more on you than you can bare. I enjoyed having my mom being at the same school I attended; however, it did have its disadvantages. In fact, I remember when I got in trouble because of chewing gum in the class, and the teacher made me place the piece of gum on my nose. It had been so long she had forgotten to tell me to take it off, and I ended up going to the cafeteria with it on my nose. Oh boy! When mom saw me come through the serving line with that on my nose, you can just imagine how scared I felt. All I can say, is mom said her usual line to me whenever we would get into trouble, which was, "If you don't straighten up, it's going to be me and you." Even though mom had to be tough with us sometimes, we always knew that she loved us unconditionally.

I recalled one day recently as I stood in the cafeteria line waiting with my students to be served lunch, memories came to me and I could just see my mom walking through the cafeteria in the back cooking area as if it were yesterday. I never felt more proud of having my mom. This reminded me of her strength, her love, her patience, her diligence, and her perseverance. I really feel this experience along with God's grace and mercy is what helped to sustain me during my own times of trials, tribulations and test of my faith.

Little did I know that the foundation I received during the early years of my life would later help to sustain my emotion and physical well-being while going through trials and tribulations, upheavals and struggles from my son Chaunce's chronic illnesses. Through my son's constant suffering I have gained patience, understanding and a belief that as hard and difficult as it may seem sometimes while going through adversities, God is there for us, he is there holding our hand when we don't even realize that he is there!!

# Introduction

In today's society and world filled with so much confusion, greed and selfishness, people are quickly forgetting about the things that are truly important in life…it is not money, it is not fame or prestige, it is not the materials things we obtain in life, and often hold so dear to us, but it is the gift of life, the possession of God's love for us. We don't realize many times how good God truly is to us. Yes, we thank him when we receive some of our blessings, or he brings us through storms and floods in our lives, but do we truly thank him and appreciate all that he has done for us.

I, myself was one of those persons who truly did not realize how blessed I was. I was taking the Lord for granted thinking that, well, if I pray during my times of trials and tribulations, the Lord will bring me out. Sometimes I believe when we begin to take God for granted, he has to put us through a test of his faith, a test of his mercy, and a test of his goodness. He also has to teach us a few things and show us who is truly in CONTROL!!! God had to take me, yes me, through a battlefield of storms in order to see if I could pass that test of faith. God sometimes have to break us down in such a way in order to let us see and realize who is actually holding us up. My course of study with God began on September 13, 1995, when he blessed us with our son, John C. Davis, II (Chaunce), who was truly a gift from God and testimony of God's goodness and mercy. Of course, I also had to endure years of prerequisites for this course of trust and test of faith. God gave us an opportunity to share in his plans for a life of a young angel sent from heaven to this earth to not only change our lives and the lives of others forever, but to also appreciate God's goodness, and enable us to surpass the material things and shallowness we surround ourselves with, and not only that, but to realize what our true purpose on this earth should be. God's plan also was for others to realize from Chaunce's living testimony that there is hope and that all things are possible when we understand that GOD IS IN CONTROL!!! This story is a testimony of how our lives were changed through the birth and life experiences of our son. It is a story about a little boy whom we knew had special needs, but through God's test of faith, we were able to realize just how special he was. So many times, throughout his life, and even before he was born, we just could not understand how this child was able to endure so much pain through the suffering of one medical hurdle after another.

My son, John C. Davis, II or Chaunce as so many of us knew him, was a little boy born with the odds already against him. Before his birth, he was given very little hope for survival; however, with God in complete control, his life was to be, and throughout his childhood, he impacted the lives of so many, regardless of race, gender or age. He was a loving child full of life, and full of hope. Despite his triumph through the birthing process, he did endure years of medical treatments, pain, and suffering. He was born with a chronic kidney disease, suffered traumatic brain injury, sleep apnea, dialysis, numerous surgeries and severe seizures. He never had the opportunity to enjoy life as most little boys do, such as playing football, basketball, soccer ball, riding a bike or taking karate lessons; however, to be with him, you never could really tell how much pain he was suffering. Sometimes he would let you know how sad he felt, and other times, he was just a cheerful little boy.

Throughout our little boy's life, God had a plan… he was here on this earth to touch, impact, and change the lives of many who knew him, and even some whom he never met. God used him as a vessel to show us that we should never give up, but have that faith the size of a mustard seed. As John's (Chaunce) mother, I was truly put through a test of faith. Sometimes our lives endured so much pain, I wanted to give up, but the Lord showed me that he was there keeping us, he was holding us up even when we did not realize that he was THERE!!!

Throughout this life experience, we struggled through storm after storm, after storm… GOD WAS THERE! When the devil was pulling at me on one side and faith on the other side, GOD WAS THERE! When family members could not and did not realize the fire we were battling through, GOD WAS THERE! When the enemy was there in my mind telling me that no one cared about our wellbeing, GOD WAS THERE! When I fell down on my knees, thinking, "Lord why are we going through so much pain, GOD WAS THERE! When we refuse to be patient and wait on the Lord to bless us, GOD IS THERE!! When we treat our enemies wrong, and become full with envy, remember GOD IS THERE!! GOD WAS ALWAYS THERE!!!

# Overwhelmed

As I reminisce about my experiences during these past few years, I have come to realize the impact my beloved son, John II (Chaunce) has had on my entire family. He's gone home to be with the Lord now, but Chaunce's presence was felt from the time he got up in the morning until the time he went to bed at night. He never let any of us experience a dull moment.

Chaunce touched many lives from the time God blessed him to be born until his untimely death at age 10. He had such a warm spirit and gentle giving personality even though he exhibited some behavior that was trying and exhausting at times. And although he had suffered much pain and had gone through constant obstacles and adversities in his life, Chaunce always had a cheerful, carefree spirit and loving attitude.

Despite his loving disposition, children began making fun of Chaunce's appearance when he was only about four years old. They made fun of him either because of the small statute he had prior to his kidney transplant or because of his thick hairy eyebrows and facial hair, his hairy arms or his older facial features caused by the medication he was taking. For no reason, children would make rude comments about him as he passed by or just stare at him rudely.

My son did not let this get his spirit down. He seemed to know that he was a child of God and I always reminded him how he was a "Miracle" – a living testimony to God's grace, mercy and his goodness. I told him that no matter what, God wanted him to be here, and God had a plan for him. I even thought about how during my seventh month of pregnancy with Chaunce, my obstetrician-gynecologist (OB-GYN), as well as the specialist she sent me to, had little or no hope for Chaunce's survival. After several tests were done, my sonogram revealed there were complications. At that time my baby seemed to have very low amniotic fluid around him and the reason for that was unknown. I was later advised to perhaps consider having the pregnancy aborted because there was no indication that the fetus had a kidney or bladder. Also, I was informed that due to such low fluid, the baby would probably have difficulty with undeveloped lungs and the hospital there wasn't equipped with the technology to help him. My husband and I were also told that he might live no longer than a few hours or a few days at the most.

This was so devastating to me and my husband. My husband seemed to begin listening to the negative reports from the doctors, but God had placed in our hearts the right thing to do. Even if Chaunce was born and only lived for a few hours or a few days, this baby had the right to do so. Even a family member one day made a comment about whether or not we had discussed funeral arrangements. I was sad when we left the hospital and went home after the tests. My husband looked at me and held my hands. He said he was by my side, and would be there for us no matter what. We could go through this together.

The things we went through seemed minute compared to the things Chaunce went through. When he was born I just hoped and prayed that the doctors' diagnosis of him having only a little part of a kidney was wrong. However, this was not God's plan. The doctors were right and the next few months were sheer stress and filled with much anxiety. But I had to remind myself that this was all in God's hand. We put our faith in the Lord and knew for ourselves that He would bring us through. Chaunce's illness helped to make our family and my marriage stronger. It also increased our faith.

When Chaunce was born, I recalled it was weeks of trials, tribulations, and uncertainties, as he lay in a tiny incubator of the ICU – Intensive Care Unit, connected to oxygen, and all types of machines and wires. The doctors and nurses tried to be positive and encouraging after having survived the unknown. Nothing hurt so much, as when I was told I had to leave my baby in the ICU because I was being discharged. I cried, and cried as I left the hospital. For days I walked up and down the halls of the hospital going to see Chaunce in the Intensive Care Unit. Having just given birth, it was not the best thing for my health. I discovered my blood pressure had elevated to stroke level and I started experiencing severe difficulties with breathing and possible heart problems. I was admitted to a hospital for further tests and observations. All I could think about was my baby was in one hospital and I was in another hospital on the other side of town. I just prayed to God to please keep my baby and watch over him. I put my cares in God's hand, because I knew at that point, no one could work it out but the Lord, and He did!! Also, during my hospital stay, something miraculous happened. During one of my Magnetic Resonance Imagings (MRIs), the technician said, "Would you look at this?" She apparently saw I had three kidneys, one left and two right kidneys, and they all were functioning fine. She informed me that normally if an individual had more than two kidneys, one of them was usually dried up and not functioning. But that was not so in my case. I knew then that God was telling me he had the right kidney Chaunce did not have, and that everything was going to be all right.

As we went through the next few years dealing with Chaunce's kidney condition, I realized that even though our lives would never be the same, Chaunce's illness made my husband grow stronger as a father. It also made my family experience things I could never imagine surviving. Most importantly, it made my marriage become stronger and helped us realize what marriage was really about. Our experience tested our love for each other, our patience and faith in God. It brought back memories of the first trial I experienced after Chaunce's birth. I remembered how we had to take Chaunce in to be checked for pneumonia, and his physician wanted him to have a spinal tap to rule out meningitis. He was only two months old and this was devastating for me and especially my husband. He truly could not stand to stay in the room and watch them place that needle into our little baby's back. Then, too, I thought I could not survive, but God gave me the strength and understanding to realize that through His goodness and mercy all things are possible.

After months of going through daily medications, diet,

restrictions, trying to keep track in my head the schedule for Chaunce's numerous medications, as well as my own for control of my blood pressure, and turmoil with Chaunce's condition not getting better, the doctors felt he needed more intervention in order to make him a candidate for a kidney transplant. They explained that Chaunce had to put on more weight in order to be placed on the waiting list. With this in mind, they wanted to train me for placing a feeding tube in Chaunce that would allow him to be fed more calories each day. This procedure involved placing him in a position where he would not move, placing a nasogastric (NG) tube down his nose until it reached a certain point in his stomach. I would then have to listen with a stethoscope and make sure it was in his stomach, because I was told if the tube accidentally entered his lungs, he would become gravely ill, and could even die of pneumonia.

The first time I had to do this procedure, I just wanted to fall down on the floor and cry for mercy. I was so terrified. I recalled looking up to God and asking, "God Why? Why does my baby have to endure so much pain?" But God gave me peace and understanding to realize this was not about me. He helped me realize all this had to be done to help my child become much closer to getting better and I shouldn't be disturbed. He let me know that he would be my strength and my guide and to just have faith. Even though I came to realize this, every time I had to complete the procedure, it tore my heart open because I had to do this while looking at my baby's face as he cried in pain and fear. I was told to get him to swallow as I placed the tube down his nose and this would help it go down much easier. This seemed to work and over the next few months God gave me the strength to do what I had to do. Throughout my son's life he would endure numerous dosages of medication, shots to draw blood … sometimes being drawn on a daily or weekly basis and pain I thought no child should have to endure. But I began to realize how truly special this child was. He had gone through more pain and agony by the time he was five-years-old than most people endured their entire lifetime. We were constantly in and out of the hospital, which we soon began calling our second home. Everyone there seemed to know Chaunce by name, and he never met a stranger wherever he went.

I remember that when Chaunce was only a few months old every time I fed him he would just throw up everything he had eaten. It was tremendously difficult for him to hold any food down. I could not go out to any events, because of this. I recalled one Sunday morning I decided to take him to church. It had been a good while since he had eaten, but I remember Chaunce was not there for more than a few minutes, when he began throwing up over everything and everyone beside me. That was when I met my longtime friend, and prayer partner. I sat beside a lady whom I had never met, named Ruby, who told me "don't worry about what he did, he is only a baby. I can always wash this dress." I seemed to feel a sense of relief at that time, and thought maybe other people out there do understand what I'm going through. From that day on I knew I had met a friend whom I will forever treasure. I explained to her about Chaunce's condition, and she seemed to be very understanding. This I knew was an angel God had sent down to earth to be with us. From then on we became very good friends even to this day.

Chaunce's doctors continued to get upset with me because of his low weight and calorie intake. I would explain to them that Chaunce would either not eat or would throw up everything he had eaten. He also seemed to have no taste for any foods (except mashed potatoes), which was on his bad list of foods to eat. I guess the low appetite was all due to his kidney condition and the fact that his body was retaining so many toxins. With my husband on the road constantly for his job, I seemed to be in this all alone. I recall being so tired and exhausted I just wanted to fall down on the floor. I would plead to God to give me strength, I would say, "Lord give me strength," and no matter how tired I was, the Lord would give me that strength to go in the kitchen and make up my baby's medication and give this to him. I just always thought my baby was on so much medication.

The test of my strength and faith in God truly came when I was told that Chaunce would have to go on dialysis. After using the NG and gastronomy tubes to increase calories and improve his kidney condition, this procedure was inevitable. The doctors told me they had put this off as long as they could. So now I thought to myself, I'm at the point of giving him so many medications every day, which I kept recorded in my head, having to give him the gastronomy-tube feedings and bolis feedings, and on top of that giving him the recommended growth hormone shots, which I dreaded, I now am going to deal with daily dialysis procedures. I just thought, giving him the growth hormone shots was so difficult because I was literally doing this by myself. With my husband being so needle shy and my daughter, Tiffani, being so young, I knew this was something I would have to do. It hurt as I gave him these shots everyday only to have him screaming and looking at me. I literally had to hold him down with one hand and stick him with the needle with the other hand. I could feel my nerves coming apart, and I just did not know how much more stress I could endure. I found myself just crying uncontrollably everyday; knowing that despite how I felt all these things had to be done. It seemed as if I was the only one who could do this, not my husband, not my daughter, not my family, just me…just me. That was when I realized God was not only keeping my son, but he was also keeping me. I thought to myself that based on research and statistics, I should not be here. After having gone through this much stress, trials and tribulations, by now I should have either have had a heart attack, stroke, aneurism or worse. That's why I know from experience how good God is!!!!! I say this to say that even though we sometimes feel we cannot endure anymore pain and suffering life has to give us, there is always strength in God. He will be there for you when no one else can or will. When you feel you cannot go a step further or about to give up because you think you cannot take anymore, DON'T, give God the chance to show you how much he loves you and prove that he is always there for us. Even though sometimes it may not seem that way, such as in my case, know that God will always make a way. He will always give you the strength you need, and he is ALWAYS THERE!!!

# God Is Always There

fter receiving training in how to do peritoneal dialysis, I got home that first night and realized I had to do the procedure with no supervision. My son's life was virtually in my hands. That was so very, very stressful and overwhelming. I remembered just sitting in a chair for a few minutes in a corner just in total shock. My husband was not able to help because he was not trained and due to the fact that this was a very sterile procedure, I had to wear gloves, mask, wash my hands constantly, etc. It was better I thought to have less people dealing with the entire process. However, it was extremely hard. This was November of 1998 and I was teaching third grade at this time. This added to the stress and pressure I was experiencing. As I look back, I had three car accidents within the time frame of a few months. My doctor told me I was under entirely too much pressure and stress, but I thought what can I do? Everything I was dealing with was out of my control. She wanted to put me on some antidepressants but I didn't feel this was a good decision. Fortunately, I did not begin the medication because in February of 1999, I discovered that I was pregnant with my youngest daughter, Karrington. Even though she was not planned, we knew it was a blessed surprise. I had often thought of having another child, but did not want to feel as though I was abandoning Chaunce or trying to make up for what I thought I had done wrong during my pregnancy with him. I believed God knew my heart and wanted us to have this second miracle.

I remember having to conduct the peritoneal dialysis on Chaunce and being so very pregnant, I could barely move around. God, I knew was still holding me up, and giving me the strength I so desperately needed. Each night of his dialysis became more and more stressful. I remembered asking myself numerous times, did I wash my hands? Did I remember to put on the mask at the right time? Did I do this; did I do that? At times, I thought I was about to lose my mind. It was such a strain on my nerves, because at the same time, I was trying to keep myself well and healthy in order to have a healthy baby. But some days, I just wanted to fall down to my knees and sob or sit by myself in a corner and cover my head. Things were beginning to take a toll on me. Each night I recalled during the first exchange, the dialysis machine would keep beeping for no apparent reason, and just as I would be about to lie down, I would have to get up and trouble shoot with the machine for about twenty or thirty minutes before it would continue. This happened almost every night. It was so nerve racking, especially during the next few months. After giving Chaunce peritoneal dialysis each night, which meant going through a five or six step process getting set up, and the next morning going through another four or five step process taking him off and recording information the doctors needed in order to monitor the procedures, such as recording his blood pressure, his weight, number of exchanges, time on, time off, it was so nerve racking. My husband was usually on the sidelines just watching or sleeping, and I guess because everything was done by me, I felt myself beginning to build resentment toward him. But I just thought that if he could help he would. God was always there to give me that needed strength and push. That faith I had the size of a mustard seed was always in my heart.

I recalled the day I had to admit Chaunce for an infection or "peritonitis" as they called it. I was informed by the doctors when we first began dialysis, that if in some way germs or bacteria enter his body during the dialysis procedure, this would occur. And not only that, but that if he got more than maybe three cases of infections, this would cause him to no longer be a candidate for a kidney transplant, which is what we were hoping, praying for, and working towards one day. I went to school to tell my administrators one morning and being met with such negative, insensitive responses, I began to cry before I even got back to my classroom. I was being pulled in all directions, my school staff did not seem to have empathy for me nor my family, and the doctors at the hospital did not want to hear that I could not be there. I knew for myself that my place was there with my son. My husband had to continue to work, and there was no other choice. My family had to come before my job, and if that meant the worse for me, so be it. My main concern was to take care of my son, my family, and also myself and unborn child.

I'll never forget the day I walked down the hall at my school on the way to my classroom. One of my school administrators passed me after being told that I was late for work because I had just had a flat tire. The comment was made," you seem to have the worst luck of anyone I know." I went on into my class and thought about what she said. I began to cry, and pray about it. I just thought to myself, "if only she knew," "if only she knew." I realized that if I just do what I can for my son and my family, God would take care of all the rest. He just kept it on my heart to pray for those who can't or won't understand. I recalled changing my son constantly everyday before leaving for work because as I would place him in the car seat in the back of the car, he would throw up. Tiffani would also be worrying me about material things, and I just remember telling her, as I was crying behind the steering wheel, that all I want is for my baby to be healthy and well, and that I am not thinking about anything else right now. I knew this was also hard on her, but I just prayed she would understand.

During the summer leading up to my child's (Karrington) birth, I experienced a true miracle. I had just been in to see Chaunce's doctors in Memphis at LeBonheur Children's Medical Center and they had told me the waiting list was very long mainly because there were so many waiting for a kidney transplant with O positive blood, and that donors with that particular blood type was in short supply. I was told the wait may be even a year to two years to find a donor match for Chaunce. Well, I remember that wonderful day, only a few days after being told this. I had left church and I had gone out to dinner with my truly good friend, and prayer partner, Ruby, and we were talking with some ladies who were eating at a table next to us. I guess they were wondering and curious as to why he (Chaunce) would not eat his food. I mentioned that Chaunce was suffering from chronic kidney disease, and he was on dialysis, while waiting for a kidney donor. We began to talk, and pray, and talk and pray. The ladies began praying a wonderful spiritual prayer asking God for this miracle for Chaunce. They could feel the pain and suffering Chaunce had endured and could sense God's blessing was on its way. Little did I know that God's miracle blessing for Chaunce was truly on the way as she had envisioned. After taking Ruby home, I went to my mom's house in Jackson, Mississippi, a town near my home in Terry, Mississippi. I had not been home in Terry all that day and did not realize that my answering machine was full of messages. The doctors from Memphis had been trying to reach me.

Dr. Baliga, who was Chaunce's nephrologist (kidney doctor) at the University of Mississippi Medical Center (UMC) was also trying to reach me. When I called them back, they gave me the wonderful news of finding a kidney donor for Chaunce and it was imperative that I get to Memphis by 9:00 p.m. that night. It was already 4:00 p.m. and my husband was out of town on a trip for his job. I thought, "How am I going to get there. Lord, what do I do now? I called my brother in law Cleavon, who Chaunce always thought of as a second dad. He was always there for Chaunce no matter what, even going on some of the trips to Memphis with us for Chaunce's checkups when my husband could not be there. He was Chaunce's Godfather in every sense of the word. He told me not to worry that he would get us to Memphis, and to just let him know when I was ready to leave. Well, I called to my pharmacy in town to let them know what was going on. I told them I needed some of my blood pressure medication and prenatal vitamins to carry me until I could get mine. They graciously said, don't worry, just come by and we'll give you what you need. I felt that God was so wonderful, just putting everything in place for us. Shortly after that, my brother in law came over to get us, and explained that he had even called to the highway patrol to inform them that he would probably be speeding, and that he was going to Memphis for a kidney transplant for Chaunce. He gave them his license plate number and they were alerted. He did in fact have to drive at high speeds in order to get us there. He was sure also to drive with his flasher on to alert the other drivers of the emergency. We then left town on our way to receive God's miracle.

As we were riding to Memphis, thoughts would flash back and forth in my mind. I would think how much we were so truly blessed to have our son, who in our hearts, was already our miracle from God. Our little Chaunce loved to play a drum beat, and he had a wonderful rhythm, and could truly play. I recalled one day when we were entering a department store, and a little boy was over in the corner playing the same tune Chaunce would beat. We just looked at each other and started to smile. Needless to say, Chaunce immediately wanted to search for the direction of that little boy playing that wonderful tune. John "Chaunce" also had this little red jacket that he just loved. It was a gift from a family member, and from the day he received it, everywhere he went he wanted to wear this jacket. I guess he just loved red, because I know for sure that his favorite power ranger was the red ranger. He wanted to wear that costume just about every Halloween.

# Satan Is Defeated

The devil is always busy and wants to ruin anything that deals with God's goodness. As we were traveling to Memphis, the devil kept putting thoughts into my head. He was saying, "Remember when Chaunce was being placed on dialysis for the first time, and how they accidentally gave him too much helpra, causing his blood to get so thin they had to give him three blood transfusions. You know that will probably cause that donor's kidney not to match."

The devil kept putting these thoughts into my head, but deep inside I knew God did not bring us all this way to leave us now. I knew that if it was in God's plan, no matter what happened with Chaunce's blood, He would make sure it will match. Even though the devil was trying to make us doubt and lose faith in God's miracle, I knew God's goodness and mercy could overshadow any doubt and disbelief the devil could ever reveal to me. He had already shown me that it would be alright, and just to continue to have faith. I had no reason to doubt my God, my Father, my Healer and my Strength.

After arriving at LeBonheur at about 8:55 that night, with only a few minutes to spare, we got checked in and the doctors and nurses began talking to us about the procedure. They did state that if Chaunce's blood type matched the donor's blood type there would be no problem. But that if they did not match, they could not perform the transplant. They stated that he was on the surgery list for 6:00 a.m. that next morning. Well, needless to say, I went to bed that night knowing I had nothing to worry about. I knew it was all in God's hand, and if it was His will, it would happen. The doctors even commented that night how Chaunce's name had moved up on the waiting list and even they couldn't explain how it happened. I just smiled because I knew, I knew how. GOD!!! They did not know what I knew, and that if it is in the Lord's plan, nothing or no one can change it. The next morning, they called to the room at 5:00 a.m. and said the tests were great and that Chaunce would have the kidney transplant as scheduled at 6:00 a.m. I looked up to God that morning and said, "Thank you Lord, thank you." Satan used every weapon he could think up to discourage me and cause me to lose my faith. I'm thankful God met me in my time of weakness, God stepped in to renew my strength and restore my faith. We should always remember to put our faith in God not in man as it speaks in the Bible. "PRAISE THE LORD, THANK YOU JESUS."

The next several weeks were taking a toll on me as well as my unborn child. I remembered having to slow down the doctor said, because of my elevated blood pressure. My doctor did not realize I was traveling back and forth to Memphis, sometimes alone, just myself and Chaunce. I would have to rent a car normally from the airport and would have to walk holding my Chaunce in one hand, and an arm full of bags in the other, just walking and waddling along eight months pregnant. Sometimes, I would become so out of breath, I could hardly speak when I got to the customer service counter. But through all this, God was there helping to hold me up, helping to give me the strength I needed, and making sure Chaunce was able to get the medical attention he so desperately needed.

A year had passed and my miracle son was beginning to enjoy life as a little boy, at least as much as he possibly could. I recalled going to his school for a class program and looking at him as he stood on the stage proudly with the other children, and just thinking to myself how blessed he was to be here and just how thankful we were to have our son. He was truly a LIVING TESTIMONY!!!

The night of September 13, 2001 will forever be imbedded in my mind as a day of tragedy. There were so many adversities and tribulations experienced in my life. My daughter Tiffani was on a drill team, which called for me to be in Jackson, approximately 45 minutes from where I live, all times of the day and night in order to support her participation. I was so exhausted at times I did not even know which direction I was heading. And I do mean this literally. My husband seemed to get upset with me for not being there for him and at the same time Tiffani was upset with me if I did not support her and stand by her side. No one seemed to care about the toll this was all taking on me. I don't even believe they realized how much it was affecting me physically, emotionally and mentally. I remember coming home to Terry one night from Jackson after leaving one of Tiffani's sporting events. I was so exhausted I could barely see my way to drive home. At that time, I had both Chaunce and Karrington in the car with me. This was something that was happening quite often. It was extremely dangerous because I was risking not only my life, but also the lives of my children and those on the road around me. I sometimes went over in the other lane or swayed from side to side of the road, I was just so sleepy and exhausted. As I came to Terry that particular night, I remember exiting off the Terry ramp. I actually sat there at the stop sign and fell asleep. The children had already fallen asleep on our way home. Something startled me and I woke up, not even realizing where I was and thinking, "Oh my God." One night, I was so physically and mentally drained that while driving home, I drove pass my turn onto my street. Before I realized it, I had driven about two miles down Tank Rd., to the next intersection, which was at the next stop sign.

When I came to myself, I had no recollection of driving pass my road. It was all a complete blank to me. "God," I kept saying, "What am I doing?" I asked God to help me as He had done so many times before." I didn't know how much more my mind and body could take. My job at school was stressful for me, also dealing with adversities there on a daily basis. I just prayed each morning before I went to work and hoped the Lord would get me through the day. I prayed to God to give me strength and guide me. However, it seemed not to be enough. What I was experiencing there was taking a toll on my strength and my sanity. On that particular night of Sept. 13, 2001, my children had been sick so I had made a late appointment with their doctor. I recalled driving home and feeling so tired and overwhelmed. I decided to give my son a bath and began running water in the tub. He said it was warm and I told him to run a little cold water in the tub. I can't believe I left him and my daughter in the bathroom with no supervision, even though he was a large child for his age of about six years old, and there was only about an inch of water in the tub. However, I realized later that it only takes a small amount of water and a few seconds for a tragedy to occur. I went to get him a towel from the laundry room and remember stopping for a minute in the kitchen and fussing at myself about things that had happened at school that day, which had me so upset and angry. After a few minutes, I returned to my bedroom, where my son was bathing and there was an awful stillness and it felt strangely quite. All I remember, is I called out and when I did, I walked into the bathtub area, and I saw Chaunce lying on his side with his face under the water, and I said "Oh my God No, Chaunce. Even though he was large in statute, I don't even remember how I got him out of the tub, other than just grabbing him up and placing him on the rug. I remember pleading to him, "Chaunce don't leave us, God, please, don't let my baby die."

My husband was not at home because his job takes him out of town. I was the only one there with the children. I remember screaming and beginning to panic. Someway, I started to perform cardiopulmonary resuscitation (CPR) on Chaunce. He looked so pale and his lips were such a dark purple. I could not get him to move, and his body felt so lifeless. I got up and ran to call 911, I remember screaming, and screaming trying to explain to the paramedic what had happened. I was almost too hysterical to give him my address. Someway, he knew the address by my phone number, and said to calm down. He said they would have someone there right away. I returned to Chaunce and finally got him to begin coughing and taking in air. When paramedics arrived, I recalled them knocking on the bathroom window and I told them to go around the house. I somehow had thought during the panic to turn off the alarm and unlock the front door. I recalled just being so hysterical and beside myself. They immediately came in and then began working on Chaunce to get him to regain consciousness. I told them I had gotten Chaunce to begin coughing and making some movement, but that he would not wake up. They worked tirelessly to get him stabilized and quickly carried him to the hospital. I told them he had an extensive medical history at UMC and to take him there. I also mentioned his kidney transplant and gave them all of his medications in a bag. I followed the ambulance and stopped to tell my husband's family, who lived down the road near us heading toward Jackson. I remember driving and frantically praying to God to help us.

When I got there I recalled seeing all of my family members and thought how everything seemed to be a dream, an awful nightmare. But I remembered how we were all outside on the sidewalk and we just stood in a circle and begin to pray for Chaunce. I recalled seeing people looking at us in a strange way, and probably wondering what we were doing. I have a close-knit family and we have always had a strong spiritual bond. I couldn't believe what was happening. They let me see Chaunce for a few minutes and he was awake and able to speak. They told me they had to run tests on him to see if he had suffered any brain damage. He seemed to know who I was and was aware of where he was. The next day while Chaunce was in Pediatric Intensive Care Unit (PICU) they ran several tests on him because for some reason he was suffering from a very high fever and the reason was unknown. After staying overnight in intensive care, I woke up and went in to see him. I saw that he was sleep and I did not want to disturb him. I had noticed that he was sleeping a great deal, but I just thought it was the medication they were giving him to keep down infection after being in the tub under water. When my husband got back in town and came by the hospital a few hours later, we went in together to see Chaunce. We noticed that everything seemed to have changed in regards to Chaunce's sense of being. He did not know who we were. He did not know my husband as his father and could not tell me what his own name was.

I immediately ran to get the nurses and doctors but the cause or reason for this was completely unknown to any of us. All they could tell me was that the tests they had completed did show a severe infection in his blood which they had began to treat with antibiotics. It became so frightening, because Chaunce would look up at the ceiling and say, "see the balloons and stars" and there was nothing at all in the ceiling. Apparently, Chaunce had suffered severe brain damage, which the doctors later told us had affected his frontal and back lobes. They said this would cause significant problems in the areas of emotions and critical thinking. Over the next few days, Chaunce was given several tests in order to determine what exactly was going on. He had seemingly lost his memory. He did not know names of his family members, how to feed himself, or even when to use the bathroom. He did not know the names of even common objects, like crayons, pencils, pillow, etc. I would show him pictures of places we would eat at like McDonald's, Piccadilly's, etc., and he could not name any of them. I would hold up a fork, and ask Chaunce what was this used for? He had no idea and could not say a word. I remember leaving out of his hospital room several times, and just bursting into tears. I was feeling so awful and guilty for leaving him in the tub that night, and just kept asking God to forgive me for what I had done. My husband and I would take turns staying at the hospital with Chaunce and I remember one afternoon when I came to the hospital after being at my school most of the day.

My husband did not know what to do or what to say. Chaunce had begun hitting the nurses who were trying to help him. He would say awful curse words at them and spit at them. We could not understand what was happening. Chaunce had always been a child who had respect for others, especially adults, and would never say bad words, or do anything to hurt someone else. I just remember holding my head in my hands and praying for my child. This little boy was no longer my "little Chaunce." His character had changed, and even his voice was not the same. Chaunce had always been so gentle and kindhearted, but he had begun pinching and hitting us and even would spit at us and slap us for no reason. He especially hit me. My sister thought that perhaps he was suffering from Tourett Syndrome, a disorder in which you make sudden, impulsive moves without thought, and for no certain reason. I just didn't know what to think or what to do at this point.

I recall going to the X-Ray room one day to have some tests done on Chaunce. He was taken there in a wheelchair, and as I positioned his lock on his wheelchair, I raised up as I was sitting in front of Chaunce, and he just slapped me for no apparent reason. He then called me the "B" word. On many occasions during the next few weeks he would just slap me in my face when it was totally unexpected and catch me completely off guard. I could not understand. All I was trying to do was help him get better. I grabbed his hand as he once more attempted to slap me and said, "You are not going to do this anymore; your hands hurt. You don't do this to me or anyone. This is not my Chaunce." He just looked and starred at me. I dreaded when the times came for him to receive his medication. He would just fight the nurses and even pinch and bite them It had gotten so bad they had to have a team of at least five nurses in order to give him his medication or draw his blood. Chaunce would sometimes call for, "Mommy," and I would say, "Chaunce, I'm right here. Mommie is here with you," and he would burst into tears. I would always hold him and console him, letting him know that God loves him and Mommy and Daddy loves him, too.

I remember taking him with me to get lunch at the cafeteria downstairs in the hospital. As I was holding his hand, a lady standing by us spoke to Chaunce, and he said "I'm going to kick your ---." I was so shocked, and embarrassed, I just said, "I'm sorry." I left out and returned to his room. I explained to Chaunce that this was very wrong and we didn't talk like that to anyone. The next day I decided to take Chaunce outside for some fresh air. As we were about to enter the elevator and the door opened, the pediatrician Chaunce had since birth was standing there. We had not seen her since the night of Chaunce's near fatal drowning. Chaunce just started crying and screaming uncontrollably. I guess it was because he could recognize her, but could not remember her name and this really upset him. Somehow I got him outside on one of the benches, where he kept crying for his mommy. I held him, saying: "Chaunce, I'm here. I love you. I love you. He kept fighting and hitting me, so I took him back to his room.

Over the next several days of tests, I was told by the doctors that Chaunce had indeed suffered severe TBI (Traumatic Brain Injury) which affected certain areas of his brain. They explained that this could be the reason for his memory loss and severe behavior disorders. I continued as I was doing such as reading stories to Chaunce and repeating phrases and songs to him in order to get him to recall information he knew. After several days Chaunce was soon able to complete a phrase or a song, if I gave him verbal prompts and cues. My husband and I saw that Chaunce was making some progress toward recovery.

During the next week, the doctors decided to admit Chaunce to the Rehabilitation Center for Children. When we got there Chaunce was afraid and did not know where he was. I recalled I had to teach Chaunce things we take for granted, such as simply washing your hands. He did not know how to use the bathroom or wash his hands. I had to tell him, how to flush the toilet and how to wash his hands step by step: Turn on the water Chaunce. Now rub the soap on your hands. Turn off the water Chaunce and get a paper towel. Rub your hands with the paper towel and throw it in the trash can. Still, I had to help him hand over hand. These were actions we think nothing about everyday, we just think we will always be able to do this with help from no one. Its like once we learn it, we don't ever think we will forget it. That first weekend we stayed at the Rehab. Center all the doctors and teaching staff were gone until Monday. I took that opportunity to continue working with Chaunce, giving him verbal prompts and cues in order to elicit responses from him. Showing various picture cards of objects, colors, letters, numbers, etc, and thanking most of all God, it all began to come back to Chaunce. Chaunce had begun to recall the names of pictured objects and words, say phrases he had learned before the accident and sing songs he had learned while in Pre-K, such as: "You are my sunshine, my only sunshine, you make me happy when clouds are gray." I thanked God for guiding us and for bringing our Chaunce back to us. On the following Monday, Chaunce was given a schedule of full day activities, such as classes for education, physical therapy, language speech therapy, and occupational therapy. He especially enjoyed recess time when he could play basketball in the playroom. I had to soon return to work, so I was able to get my sister Lillie who had the experience of a registered nurse to stay with him. My daily schedule was a very rigorous and hectic one and began with my getting up at 3:30 a.m. to get Chaunce's personal items prepared for the day. As he continued to sleep, I would go down the hall and take a shower and get dressed. After my sister arrived at 5:30, I would leave to go to my mom's house where Karrington was staying. I would wake Karrington (who was about two-years-old at that time), bathe her, dress her for school, and get her there between 6:15 to 6:30. I would then head to the school where I worked to make it there by 7:00 a.m. I would work, spending that full day teaching my Multiple

Disabilities Class. Here I would teach between 6-8 students, who were all in wheelchairs, reading and language skills. With the majority of the students being severely disabled, I would also feed and change them while completing other daily teaching tasks. My job was a blessing to me, and I guess because of my Chaunce's medical condition, I could genuinely relate to my parents and what they were probably going through. Some of my babies, which I often called them, were non-verbal and some could not even use their hands. After getting my students on their school bus at the end of the day, I would leave to pick up Karrington, and try to spend at least some part of the day with her. I knew she was only two-years-old and did not understand anything that was going on, other than her big brother was not around her for some time. I would then return to the Rehab Center and spend the remainder of the afternoon and evening with Chaunce, reviewing what he had learned that day, and getting him to tell me what things he had experienced and remembered. I would continue to work with him on skills until bedtime, as well as pray with him and sing two of his favorite songs he had learned in Pre-school and was once again able to remember.

After finally getting a few hours of sleep, I would again start my daily ritual of getting up at 3:30 a.m. and going through the day. This continued for two weeks. My husband, who worked so hard to maintain his job also, had no idea what stress and trials I was facing daily. I did not want him to be on the road worrying about us, and I knew he was doing all he could. This I knew was truly a test of our faith and trust in the Lord. And even though I did have some days, I just wanted to roll up in a knot in the corner and cry from sheer physical and mental exhaustion, I knew I had to be there for our son, he was the one who I knew had really suffered. I just prayed to God to give me strength and he did. I began to talk to God more and more, and put all my cares on him. I remembered what the Bible says, "That he will not leave us nor forsake us." I knew for a fact then that these were true words spoken.

Our son was finally released from the Rehabilitation Center. The next several months were a time of uncertainty, and true learning experiences for our son. Chaunce had began regaining some of his memory but still had difficulty remembering some family members' names and names of places we had gone before his brain injury. I'll never forget the first day we got home from the hospital; Chaunce looked over at me, before we got out of the car and said, "Mom, what do I do now?" I just thought to myself, we take one day at a time, and lean on the Lord. He's our strength and our guide. I thought for a moment to myself, and realized that my baby literally meant, "What does he do now?" He had no sense of getting out of the car and going into the house. Our son looked so lost and frighten. I felt so much pain and hurt for him. I recalled saying to Jesus, our son has suffered so much in his life time, and I just don't understand or know the reason he has to experience so much pain and turmoil.

The next few months were difficult roads to recovery. Chaunce had continued to regain his memory in daily living tasks, learning and remembering his basic academic skills, which before the accident, he was so smart and bright in Math, Reading, and Language, and now I realized all this had changed, and I knew this was such a challenge for him. Many days, I noticed Chaunce just sitting and starring. I knew he was sitting there thinking about so many things, and just did not know how to put his thoughts into words. This was so frustrating and devastating for him. Even though I was also upset, I tried not to let Chaunce see this on my face, and just remembered looking to God and thanking him for not taking our son and allowing him to remain on earth with us. I knew it could have been the opposite and Chaunce could not have even been here. My husband and I did feel so blessed and thankful for God's goodness and mercy.

After months of struggling to learn to write again, Chaunce was once again able to write legible words. When he first attempted to write, he could only make lines and unrecognizable marks. I decided to place him back at the preschool program he had graduated from the previous May, because the class size was small and he would be able to receive more one on one instruction from his teacher. I knew at this point of his life that it was crucial and would help limit his level of frustration. The teacher at the Rehabilitation Center was great in helping coordinate the instruction for Chaunce. She was able to target certain strategies useful in helping Chaunce become successful in his instruction using techniques for teaching students who have suffered Traumatic Brain Injury (TBI). I know this all took so much patience from his teacher and being a teacher of special needs children, I especially realize this was a key component in his recovery. In the evenings, I would work with Chaunce one on one to increase his level of understanding. Chaunce continued to make progress and regained the majority of his reading and language skills. He continued; however, to experience great difficulties in math and any area dealing with critical thinking skills or completing things through a process of steps. His doctors told me this was to be expected due to his injury. Chaunce was also able to continue receiving his speech language therapy and occupational therapy, which he had received in the Rehabilitation Center. He received therapy twice per week, and my husband would normally come in town from his job and take him to his therapy sessions. I realized this was extremely difficult and exhausting for my husband, but he agreed to do this if it meant Chaunce would be able to improve. It gave Chaunce and his dad an opportunity to bond and reestablish their relationship.

During the next few months to a year, we were not able to take Chaunce anywhere like the mall or grocery store or have him unattended. He had to be taken by the hand everywhere. I realized this the day when I took Chaunce to a store and had him standing by me. I turned to put something back on the stand and he disappeared. I frantically searched for him for several minutes before going to the store's customer service to have his name paged on the public intercom system. I thought to myself, that he probably would hear his name, but would not know how to ask for help. A few minutes later I found Chaunce and from that point on I remembered and told my husband not to ever leave Chaunce unattended if he had him out in public, not even for a second. Due to his traumatic brain injury, he did not have any sense of right or wrong when it came to his safety. He almost stepped out in front of a car one day and from that day on I learned to hold his hand whenever we were out. I was so afraid for him when he was not with us. I was terrified for him to go out on field trips at school. I just told the teachers to let me know when they had a trip planned, and I would schedule to go with them. Due to the traumatic brain injury, Chaunce had a very difficult time dealing with emotions. I remembered the day I took him to a Toys R Us Store. He wanted a toy which I did not think he needed, because it was not appropriate for him. He literally cried, had a falling down, screaming tantrum in the middle of the parking lot, and I did not know at first how to react. It took all my strength to get him into the car. I guess people thought I was the worst mother the way they were looking and staring at us.

During the course of the next few months, I continued to help Chaunce grow and recall memories of the past. With God's grace and mercy Chaunce continued to get better, and I know for a fact that God never leaves you nor forsakes you. We decided to place Chaunce into public school the next school year. He had regained a great deal of his memory and retained the skills he needed to complete the majority of his class work. I placed him in the kindergarten program at the school where I taught. He still had some difficulty with any skill dealing with critical thinking, but most of all, the first few weeks of going to a public school indicated he had extreme difficulty with his social skills. I guess being in a public school for the first time, especially after just having suffered a brain injury, made the adjustment for him that more difficult. Every day for the first three weeks, Chaunce would come in through my classroom door, and within a matter of minutes he would throw up everywhere. I would have to clean him up before he went on to class. I realized it was not a virus or any type of illness, but that he was suffering from anxieties. He really hated and feared going to breakfast without any assistance and being around so many students. He was always used to a small school environment, where his entire class (of only about five to six students) would go to the cafeteria and eat breakfast and lunch together. Realizing this, I quickly worked out a schedule with his teacher and the cafeteria staff, and Chaunce was able to adjust and continue making progress throughout the remainder of the school year.

John "Chaunce" loved basketball. That was his favorite sport, even though he could not play the game with anyone one on one. Due to this kidney condition, as well as, his traumatic brain injury he could not participate in any contact sports. I remembered the time we got the kids an indoor basketball court, similar to that you see at Chuck-E-Cheese, and Karrington and Chaunce would play sometimes for one or two hours non-stop. A few months later my husband and Chaunce had gone over to my sister-in law's home where her son who was four years older had challenged Chaunce at scoring some basketball points. Little did he know that Chaunce had been playing a perfect game. When Chaunce started playing the game and throwing the ball in the goal non-stop, they could not believe it. My husband just stood by the side and smiled, because he knew something they did not know. Chaunce just kept throwing the ball and laughing. I even recalled sometimes when Chaunce and I would go to the doctor's office for a visit, and while waiting for the doctor, Chaunce would challenge me to a ball of paper and waste can competition. Wow!! When he would beat me, he would get so tickled. I remember those wonderful times that we did share.

Sometimes I just would sit and think to myself, what can I do to become a better parent, a better mother? What am I doing so wrong to cause me to endure so much pain and heartache? I know these experiences I have had does not seem normal to me or anyone else. I remind myself that I can't question God's will and I can't lean to my own understanding. Perhaps God is trying to show me something and He is using my son and family to make that point with me. I even feel sometimes that maybe he is trying to help others through me. I must remember what the Bible says, "cast your burdens on the Lord and he will sustain you," Psalm 55:22. I must allow myself to do this because I feel once I give my burden to God and stop trying to solve or understand what is going on in my life, and my family's life, maybe he will begin to reveal to me his purpose for all the tragedy and suffering we are enduring.

Sometimes my life seems to be going OK, but then it takes a turn and becomes even more painful than I could imagine. I went through the agony of completing the National Board of Certification process. This took several months of preparation, and I experienced sheer stress and anxieties, as well as, having all kinds of obstacles placed in my way, such as having many of my materials lost, or unaccounted for and dealing with the thought of not being able to complete the process even after I had poured my heart and soul into this entire procedure. Upon my completion of this experience, which took a toll on me physically, emotionally, and mentally, I went in for my scheduled routine mammogram. I had no real concern about it and just knew the results would be normal. But to my surprise my test indicated a possible sight of cancer on my right breast. My heart started beating a mile a minute. I was told that it may be a lip node and I needed further tests.

The next few months before my tests, I found myself praying to God and asking Him why I had to endure turmoil after turmoil. I did not mention this to my family and only told my husband weeks later, just before my tests. I cried and worried, and worried and cried, until I just couldn't cry anymore. I just couldn't imagine what would happen to my family and especially Chaunce, if something were to happen to me. I had to pull myself together and remember to put my cares in the Lord's hand. I knew that even though I had no idea of my fate, the Lord had already ordered my steps and this was all in his hands. I began to pray, and just said, Lord, whatever is your will. I know you have always said you will not leave me nor forsake me. I know whatever is to happen is your will. I had no control of what was to be. **"PRAISE THE LORD"**, the next mammogram I received showed that it was only a lip node, benign, and everything seemed to look normal. I remember, thanking God when I was told this wonderful news. I left the clinic, went out to my car, putting my hands and head on my steering wheel, and crying like a baby, just thanking God, and praising the Lord for his goodness and mercy. I kept saying thank you God, thank you; God thank you. I knew this was only through God's mercy that the outcome was a positive one. I called my husband and told him about my joyous news, and he too was so thankful. My son Chaunce's life was trying to get better, with some of his loss of memory problem getting better, but due to the damage to his brain, which controlled your emotions, his behavior was getting worst. I decided to take him to be placed on medication for behavior because he continued to pick on and abuse Karrington. I often thought to myself, "what could I do?" I can't leave my husband and Chaunce and take Karrington to live somewhere else. I couldn't leave Chaunce with anyone else. Lord, what should I do is all I thought to myself. After he was placed on medication for his behavior problems, a couple of weeks passed, and I only saw a very small degree of improvement. However, I did begin to notice another problem. He began having seizures, which were sometimes very severe. We were never able to determine how or why he began having them. The next several months entailed seeing neurologists after neurologists, having numerous tests done to determine the cause, and what exactly was going on when he was having the seizures. He was placed on seizure medication to help control them. The first night he had a seizure. He was in the bed with me, and began shaking and trembling. I did not know what was going on at first, but I quickly remembered what had happened in my class sometimes when some of my students in my special needs class would have seizures, and determined that was what Chaunce was experiencing. I called 911 and they had an ambulance and paramedics there in a matter of minutes. We continued to monitor Chaunce and give him medical attention. The problem we seemed to be faced with was that he was on so much medication from his kidney transplant to fight rejection of his kidney. We were just limited in what we could give him for treatment of his seizures.

At first, Chaunce had seizures only at night, but all of a sudden, he began having uncontrollable seizures for no apparent reason, even at the sound of any sudden noise. It could be a bell ringing, the alarm being set, the timer on the oven, and strangely enough, even my husband's watch was ticking one day, and Chaunce just dropped his glass of milk, and loss his balance. These seizures were so dangerous because you never knew when he would hear a sound or sudden noise. It was as if he was hypnotized. He would fall out and lose control of his body completely. He had no way of controlling this because he would just fall backward or forward whenever he heard the slightest sound. I remember him falling in the kitchen one day and hitting his head on the wall very hard. I was coming out of the laundry room at home, and the oven alarm went off. I could not get to him in time, and he just fell backwards. My poor son suffered so many falls, bumps, and bruises to his head and his face, but neither we nor his doctors could understand what was causing this behavior. The doctors decided to admit him into the hospital to have tests done to try to determine what was happening, but this all proved unsuccessful, and the falls continued to occur. His seizure medications were increased, but still even this did not seem to help much. It was so frightful for Chaunce to go anywhere because we did not know when or where a sound would trigger this seizure episode. It had gotten so severe that his neurologist prescribed a helmet, which they said needed to be worn constantly. Chaunce wore his helmet, but sometimes we had difficulty in getting Chaunce to keep it on. I would look around and all of a sudden Chaunce would have taken off his helmet.

The strangest thing happened though with his uncontrollable seizures. As strange and sudden as they came about, they all of a sudden stopped the same way, but not before Chaunce experienced numerous more serious falls and bruises. He did continue to have the grandma seizures, which would occur mostly at night as he was sleeping. And as the uncontrollable behavior continued with Chaunce, so did the seizures. He continued to physically and mentally abuse Karrington calling her horrible names. I later realized he might be taking it out on Karrington when children called him names or just as he did when I spanked or disciplined him. He would get mad and upset and turn and punch Karrington for no reason. My life day in and day out was a constant challenge or to me like a war zone, and there seemed to be no relief or end in sight. Ninety percent of the time my husband was not around for one reason or another and when he was around, he still did not give much assistance with discipline at all. He seemed to look at me whenever the children were acting up as if I were the only adult around to give a spanking or discipline. He just did not respond, especially the way I felt a strong father figure should. He continued to leave all the discipline to me, and then would wonder why Chaunce seemed to resent me so much.

One day I was at a beauty salon and barbershop to get my hair done and I had both of the children with me as I usually did. Chaunce asked for something out of the vending machine, which I felt he did not need to eat. He became so upset with me that he was literally trying to, well not trying to, but actually fighting me. He hit me and when I disciplined him, it only got worse. The men on the barber shop side had to get on him and tell him, "Son you don't hit your mother." I was so upset, embarrassed, and stressed to the limit. I had to remind myself of his brain injury as possibly being the cause for his behavior. But, it still hurt my heart that he would do that to me, especially after all the things I had done to care for him. I often think how awful I must be as a parent. All I ever tried to do was to help my children. But I only thought to myself how dysfunctional we as a family seemed to be to other people. People I believe probably thought we were living a good life. We seemed to have money, a nice home, good jobs, security, etc. But if only they knew how much pain my family was suffering. How inadequate I felt as a parent, stressed, depressed, and on the edge of suicide the majority of the time. When I was out in public, I always tried to keep a smile on my face, but people around me at work, at my church, just did not realize how I was crying for help so much on the inside, and needed to talk to someone who would listen and understand. The pain and suffering Chaunce was going through with his major medical ordeals, chronic kidney disease, traumatic brain injury, seizures, which could not seem to be controlled, and even now sleep apnea, I would find myself on my knees and on the floor, crying Lord help us, Lord help me!!!! It had gotten to the point that I was afraid to leave Karrington alone in the house anywhere without my supervision. I remembered the day I could not find Karrington, and I was running crazily through the house calling her name Karrington, Karrington where are you?, and asking Chaunce, where is Karrington. She did not answer me at all, and I was afraid something awful had happened to her. She finally came out from beside of the buffet in the dining room and was in the corner hiding because she had done a bowel movement in her pants. I did apologize to Chaunce, because I did not know if he had done something to her or what. I was just about crazy out of my head with paranoia. I even remembered one night when I had stopped to get the children some hamburgers to eat. I had gotten a good ways down the highway, and Chaunce said he did not have his burger, only fries. I said, Chaunce are you sure they are not in your bag. He said, no they are not in here. I frantically turned around and had to go back almost two miles to the restaurant, and as I was about to get out of the car, he said, I think I already ate it. I was so upset with him and already so terribly exhausted, I just wanted to scream. I held on to my steering wheel and made a loud grunting sound. I was so tired of always having to hold in my frustration. My husband did not have any idea what pressure I was under. I knew our son needed help and I was determined to get him the help he needed. My husband did not seem to realize the magnitude of the problem because he was either gone or due to his bad hearing, could not hear the awful things Chaunce was saying to Karrington or even to me. I felt a great deal of the time he was just ignoring what he suspected was going on to keep from having to deal with it. I remember the day I decided to have Chaunce admitted to a behavioral hospital for observation, as well as, treatment, I knew his dad would be totally against it. I felt that he needed professional help, which I was not able to give him, and my Karrington needed a break from the years of mental, physical, and emotional abuse she was enduring on a daily basis. When I went home to get Chaunce's clothes, my husband quickly asked, where was he? I told him where he was and why. He did not and would not understand the situation. He just said I seemed to be the one with the mental problem, and that I was the one who needed help. His response was one I expected, because he never had realized or admitted there was a problem. I remember all the way back to the hospital he did not speak one word to me, it was total silence in the car. When we got back to the hospital, I recalled, Chaunce was pleading with us to take him home, and the caretakers were holding him away from us. I could see the anger in my husband's face. Needless to say, Chaunce was not there for more than a day. He came home with us the following day, and the emotional and mental abuse continued.

I even remembered when we were coming home from a visit for Chaunce in Memphis, and I reached to get a bottle of sanitizer, or so I thought. When I looked at the bottle, it was all black and I said, what is this? I did not know at the time what to think. A few days before Chaunce had gotten upset with Karrington, and apparently played a trick on her. He had gotten her black foam off of her play microphone and had stuffed in into the bottle of sanitizer. Therefore, when I reached to get it, not knowing what he had done, I was in shock. This was one of the many jokes he would play sometimes on Karrington.

My poor Karrington suffered the name calling, emotional, physical, and mental abuse daily. With Chaunce constantly around her she could get absolutely no relief. I knew my baby girl's self esteem was diminishing little by little. I felt so helpless with no true support from my husband or my family at that point. It had gotten so awful and severe with her that she was beginning to have wetting and bowel movement accidents on herself. She even had gotten to the point that she had picked up a strange habit, and I knew that this all had to do with her being abused daily by her brother. I noticed that she had begun eating dirt and dust. Everywhere she saw dust or dirt, the vacuum, furniture, the tv, etc., she would rub her fingers on it and put it in her mouth. I would see her and try to discourage her from doing this. Many times she would just deny she was doing it. I knew that she should know better because she was already four or five years old, and she never had done this before. It even got to the point of her eating laundry detergent. I would sometimes catch her in the laundry room at home and I say, "Karrington what are you doing?", and she would say nothing, but I could tell immediately that she had been eating washing detergent from the box.

Things had gotten so bad at school Karrington and Chaunce attended because Chaunce would still call her terrible names, and even have the other children at school picking on her, calling her names, emotionally abusing her, etc., that she was having daily bowel movement accidents on herself and would not say that she had done it. Everyday, I picked her up and she would just look at me and began to cry. Others could not understand what was wrong, but I knew my poor little girl had to get away, somehow, SOMEHOW!! That was when I decided to take Karrington out of the school with Chaunce and put her at another school away from him and his terrible abuse of her. The other school was across town from Chaunce's school and my job, but I would get up early every morning before 5:00 a.m. to get us all where we had to be. By the time I finally got myself to work, I was exhausted before my day even began, but I would give my students in my class all that I had.

Even though she did improve somewhat, she was still having to be exposed to her brother's abuse on our way home and while we were at home. I could not leave them alone for a second. I was so drained trying to keep my eyes on them constantly, and at all times. He would say things to her like, Karrington you are a punk; you fagot, just horrible names for anyone to hear. He would yell out, Karrington you are so stupid. He even talked about killing her and saying "I wish you were dead." Every time I would come around them, he would just deny saying or doing anything like that, but I knew it had happened. I was even able to catch him one day, when I was in the kitchen and he did not realize I was next to the room they were in, the family room, and I heard what he said. I sat down on the couch and talked with him and asked him, why are you always so mean to your baby sister. I would tell him that she was like a jewel, and he was a lot older than her and should be protecting her from other children. I mentioned that a jewel was precious and that he shouldn't treat her ugly in anyway.

I got so upset one day when I was talking with Karrington, and she told me Chaunce had stuck her with a knife on her leg, and when I looked on her thigh and did see a small abrasion which could have been a knife cut, I told my husband. Just as usual, he did not do anything. This made me that more upset with him and the verge of divorce. All I could think about was that I had to take Karrington away, and just leave. We could not stay here anymore. Many times I just wanted to leave, but how could I leave Chaunce? What would happen to him and who would care for him? I just would always say, **"LORD, HAVE MERCY, LORD HAVE MERCY ON MY SOUL, LORD, PLEASE GIVE ME STRENGTH,"AND HE WOULD.** All this stress was on me, and Tiffani our oldest daughter, was away at college, so she was literally no help. If she would come home, she would only make matters worst. She and Chaunce definitely did not get alone at all. She would try to discipline him, and he would begin to fight with her. That would make her even madder, and she would say, "mom just let you have your way because of your medical problems." Tiffani just did not realize that Chaunce truly loved his mother. He hated when Tiffani would argue with me, and he would become very upset. He did not even like it when my husband and I would raise our voices in conversations. He would tell Tiffani, I remember, "leave my mom alone, come on mom, come on." She would not understand about what traumatic brain injury does to your emotions or even your logical way of thinking. She would hit him or spank him, and he would hit her back, they would go back and forth until he just threw up over everything. Sometimes, I could tell when that was about to happen, and get him outside in time. Other times, when I didn't, he would make a mess and I would just tell her or him, one of you had better clean it up. This was why I would say to myself, Tiffani could help when she wanted to, but many times, I would just rather her not be around him. I told her once that she must be embarrassed or ashamed of us, because, whenever, we all went out together, to the mall, or the movies, she would distance herself from us, and go in the opposite direction. She just did not realize she had issues too. Whenever, she called me from college, she only seemed to bring me more stress and heartache. I just couldn't take any more. I just wanted to leave this world. Death was not frightening to me anymore. I did not care at that point, if I lived or died. But I didn't want to leave my children behind. That was what kept me from thinking the worst, from doing the worst thing, which was taking my own life.

I'll never forget the night I got home and was met with a surprise. I had had a long stressful day at work and after leaving choir rehearsal that evening I got in the truck with the Karrington and Chaunce. I had just taken a break from the chaos Chaunce and Karrington would always have me going through trying to be a referee for them constantly. I seemed to be less burdened when I went to church and gave my cares to the Lord. I would find myself often crying and upset as we sang our songs of praise. Again, people around me, such as my family, choir members, my co-workers, etc., knew my son had medical problems, but they did not know the magnitude of our problem. They did not realize the stress and the turmoil I was facing daily. I would just smile and keep things to myself. I would think to myself, if I can't get my own husband and family to help us, how could I expect other people to care or take the time to help me deal with my problems?

Our family situation had gotten so stressful and to the point that one night, I could not take it anymore. I began to cry uncontrollably. He (my husband) did not even see me leave out of the front door all upset. He didn't even notice that I was gone. I found myself driving and crying, not knowing or realizing where I was going. All I could think of was that I was ready to end my life. As I drove down the dark and narrow country road, I cried and cried until I began feeling the left side of my body become num and very weak. I swayed across the road and nearly went off in the ditch toward some trees. I drove until I ended up at my sister and her husband Cleavon's house in Jackson and when I entered their home they asked me what was the matter, I just broke down and fell to the floor crying, screaming and sobbing. I recalled shouting to them to help me, LORD HELP ME!!! I realized then that I was on the edge of a nervous breakdown. With all the stress in my life and no one to really talk to or even give me relief from caring for Chaunce and Karrington, not only his chronic medical problems, but his mental illness as well. I had just gotten to the point where my body and my mind were ready to give up. I no longer had a fear of death. My pastor one day saw how stressed I was and sat down and talked with me. He spoke to me with some true words of encouragement. He stated that if I had gone off the road the night that I wanted to take my life, and hit a tree, what would have happened if I did not die, but rather survived the crash with paralysis. Without being able to care for myself at all I would then need someone to care for me. That he said, would cause that much more stress on my family and me. He was right, I had not thought about it that way. I could not bare having to have someone care for me, feeding me, dressing me, changing me, etc. That helped me to open my eyes and realize that I could not give up, I JUST COULD NOT GIVE UP!!

On my way home one night, Karrington cried for some cookies I had in the truck. I told her she could not get them and did not need them. I'll say for about eight miles, she cried and had a tantrum. Disciplining her did not seem to help at all, especially while I was trying to drive. Chaunce was continuing to pick on her as well, and I was telling him to hush. I guess I just loss it and started screaming at both of them. I suppose I really frighten them, because they finally got very quiet. I remember going down I-55 highway for miles, just crying to myself, and trying to see the road through my tears. When I got home, I was met with an awful surprise. I came in through the back door at my house, because there was a delivery left at my front door, which blocked us from getting in. I'll never forget what I saw as I came through the kitchen into the family room. I looked over at the wall in the far corner, which I did often as I came in to see the time on the clock on the wall. I looked down on the floor; my eyes seemed to be drawn downward. I saw a long, black snake stretched out along the corner wall. I just wanted to scream out, but I knew if I did, it would frighten the snake and the children.

I immediately ran and got a broom, and told the children to bring me the telephone. As I held the broom on the snake so he could not crawl away, I called my brother-in-law to come and help me. My husband, as usual was out of town, and it was only me there to deal with this. I was trying so hard to keep the snake from crawling into a closet that was nearby. I was so terrified and frightened. I could feel my nerves drawing tighter and tighter. I have never been more frantic and upset in my life, as I was that night. I can deal with many things, but seeing a snake in my house is just not one of them. I just wanted to fall down on the floor once things had settled down and burst into tears. Chaunce was at home with his dad the day before, and he had a bad habit of coming in the house and not closing the front door completely. Just the thought of knowing the snake was in the house over night and all that day brought tears to my eyes. I was shaking all over my body and began having an anxiety attack.

Minutes after we had gotten the snake out of the house, I was in the dining room vacuuming. Karrington wanted to help and when I told her not right now, I heard a loud pop noise but did not know at the time what it was. I later realized as I got around to the other side of the dining room that there was shattered glass all on the floor. I looked up and saw that one of my favorite and expensive pictures had the glass broken and shattered on the floor in front of it. I looked near it and found one of Karrington's toys. I discovered at that point that she was so upset that she could not vacuum, that she had apparently thrown one of her toys across the room and obviously thrown it so hard it broke my picture's glass. I just wanted to shake her, but I was so upset, I just said, "Karrington, go to bed right now!!! I knew if I had to discipline anyone at this point, I would probably just lose it.

I stopped vacuuming and sat down to the dining room table holding my head. I thought to myself, it can't get any worst than this tonight. I thought, "My God, what else can possibly go wrong?" Well, I was wrong. The telephone rang and it was Tiffani. I knew it was bad because she began by saying "Mom, promise me you won't get mad with me." I immediately said, "Tiffani, what is it?" I did not even mention to her about the day I had had or finding the snake in the house. She began to say that while she was up to my house visiting us just before her college dorm opened back up, she had left her flat screen computer in her friend girl's apartment and while she was gone, someone had broken into her apartment and stolen Tiffani's computer. I just started screaming at her saying, remember how I kept trying to get you to let me bring it up to my house until your dorm opened and you were ready for it. It was already boxed up, and would not have been any trouble doing that. I even offered to bring it back to her. But she kept saying, "I will take care of it myself, mom". "Well, you sure did, I told her." I was so angry at her.

Rita B. Davis

I had only bought the computer five months earlier, and was still paying for it. I later found out that the computer was stolen and sold to someone else. I just wanted to come through that telephone and shake Tiffani, because I knew this was something that could have been avoided. In fact, it had been months and months, and I had not even told my husband. I just knew he would have had a major fit. I remember that night so clearly. I was so upset and frantic that I sat up all night. I didn't close my eyes even once. Between Chaunce, Karrington, Tiffani, and the snake, I was just about on the edge of a breakdown. I could feel myself having one anxiety attack after another. I sat there all night watching my feet, looking round, and wondering if there could be another snake somewhere in the house. I cried and cried and cried and just said "Lord, I just can't take anymore, I can't take it anymore." My husband called me at about 3:00 a.m. and I told him about the welcome I had when I got home, and how the snake nearly frightened me to death. I was so upset with him and believe me he knew it. I told him how I had been sitting up all night long and could not go to sleep. The next morning after we left the house, and while I was driving up the highway to work, I guess I had another anxiety attack, and burst into tears. I cried, cried, and cried. I could not let my feelings about the snake come out that night before because I was afraid of scaring the children, as well as, the snake. So I had no choice except to hold it all in. I suppose the drivers passing by me probably thought I was losing my mind. Well, the way I felt, they would not have been too far off base. I just could not hold my frustration in any longer, all my stress, all my turmoil, anger and suffering surfaced.

For the next several days, I just thought about all the tragedy my family and I seemed to have suffered, dealing with one death after another. First, was my mother in law's death...she passed all of a sudden one Sunday morning and I just remember the pain I felt as I informed my husband. He was out of town when she passed, so telling him this dreadful news upon his return home was something I never thought I would have to do. I know losing a loved one is difficult and losing your mother and not being there when it happened is even more painful. My husband looked at me, as if in disbelief. When I told him I just tried to console him and let him know that his mother was now in God's care. I wanted him to understand that we have no control when it is in God's hands. During the next several months, I had experienced the death of two of my choir members. They were also very special people to me. It seemed as if I was going to one funeral after another. I was becoming so overwhelmed and just did not realize it. In December, I learned that one of my former student's mom had passed away. I remembered her so well, and it just hurt my heart hearing about this news. I will never forget that day because I was stressed out of my mind with one ordeal after another.

One day we got out of the truck and Chaunce did not want to wear his helmet. I made him put it back on constantly, but somehow, we got inside the store and Chaunce was without his helmet. I had gone to a neighborhood store to return some towels, running late for my own doctor's appointment, I planned to take only a few minutes to do this. Well, I told Chaunce and Karrington to stay near me and do not walk off from me, which they would sometimes do. I felt if something was to sound off loud, I would be near Chaunce and maybe I would be able to catch him before he would fall. As soon as I turned my head to pick up a new towel, Chaunce and Karrington both disappeared from me. The next thing I know, I heard my name being announced on the public address system in the store, requesting that I come to the ladies' dressing room. I got there and the first thing I saw was Chaunce sitting down in a chair and Karrington standing behind him. They both looked frighten out of their skin. Chaunce had a lump on his forehead the size of an apple it seemed. He didn't even look like himself. The store staff insisted that I let them call for emergency personnel. Well, they did, and a group of about 10-12 paramedics and firefighters showed up to see about him and take him to the hospital. This was something I felt did not have to happen if only Chaunce had kept on his helmet and if they both had followed my instructions and not left my side. I was very upset with them and they knew it. However, I was glad it wasn't more serious.

As I was leaving the store with Chaunce and Karrington, one of my former co-workers informed me that the mother of one of my former students had passed that day. I was very upset about that news because it was a parent I had talked to often, perhaps because her child was disabled and I was going through that similar experience with Chaunce's disabilities. We often talked for hours and consoled one another. We both knew God was giving us strength to take care of our precious angels. I broke down in tears just crying on my way to the hospital. I just could not believe she was gone. The doctors at the hospital wanted to keep Chaunce overnight because they wanted to monitor his kidney functioning and his seizure disorders. That was about 1:00 p.m. that afternoon and we were in the Emergency Room until about 7:00 p.m. I was so tired and drained. There was a problem and delay in getting his room ready and I became upset with the hospital staff. I had to call my husband and let him know where we were, and then he was upset. This was so overwhelming and just another level of stress added onto my already mountain of stress. I felt Chaunce had learned from this experience and now realized that he must obey and be aware of the dangers when he does not. I explained to him that this could have been fatal, especially with him already having suffered a traumatic brain injury. I noticed his blood pressure would not go down, it remained elevated and the doctors had to give him medicine to help bring it down. The doctors and I jokingly said it could be that he was afraid of what I might do to him for not obeying me in the first place. However, I let him know that I was upset, but that I was more relieved that he would be ok. I knew it could have had a much more serious outcome, if it had not been for the Lord watching over him.

That next weekend, I was about to go to the funeral family hour for the mother of my student that had passed, when I learned that Cleavon, who was Chaunce's godfather, and the one I could always count on and call on whenever we needed his help, had just passed. Apparently, he had difficulty breathing and died in the ambulance while on his way to the hospital. I always felt that Cleavon was more than a brother-in law. In fact, he was the one who had taken Chaunce and I to Memphis for his kidney transplant when my husband was not in town, and had taken us there several times after that for numerous checkup and appointments in Memphis. It seemed as if he was always there. He was truly God's tower of strength for Chaunce and myself, always being there with words of encouragement, and just being that type of person everyone looked to for advice about anything, and I mean anything. We always called him a walking encyclopedia. This was the day before Christmas Eve.

The next day as I was attending the funeral services for the little student's mother from my classroom, I later found out that my husband's brother had just passed. So within that one weekend, I had lost two brother-in-laws. Even though they had both been battling with chronic illnesses, it just did not make their deaths feel any less painful for us to bear. I remembered going to the funeral home to see my two brother-in-laws. Yes, they were at the same funeral home and that experience was so overwhelming. I saw them both just lying there and remembering the times we had all shared was so difficult for the entire family. We were able to make it through the week and now were preparing to attend the two funerals of our loved ones on the same day. We had struggled to get the funerals held at different times, but were not able to make that happen. My husband had desperately wanted to attend both funerals, because he was very close to Cleavon, as well, and he was having a very difficult time dealing with not only his brother's death, but that of Cleavon's. In fact, he mentioned to me when I arrived home that night that he was just sitting on the side of our bed, still in disbelief about Cleavon when he got the call about his brother, Bill. We ended up going to each funeral, both at 11:00 a.m. My husband of course attended his brother's, and I decided to attend Cleavon's funeral, because he was such an important part in not only my life, but also in Chaunce's life. He always called Chaunce, "His little buddy." Chaunce was also having a very difficult time dealing with his death, and it was taking a toll on him during that week. Due to Chaunce's brain injury which affected his ability to deal with emotions, he just had an even more difficult time dealing with the death of someone who meant absolutely so much to him. We explained the conflicts to the families, and they all seemed to understand our difficult situation.

Later that day I went to be with my husband's family at the repasse for his brother. I thought it was so amazing that day as we prepared to board the family cars at Cleavon and my sister's house. Many of the family members had met there, and we decided to make a circle outside in the yard before getting into our cars to say a prayer that God would give us strength. Suddenly, as we were praying a great burst of wind blew over our heads and we knew that was a sign from Cleavon letting us know he was there with us. He was witnessing all of the love that was shown to him during this sad time of his death. God had even blessed us with such an array of sunshine, and was now bringing that back to us, because the day before was cloudy with inclement weather. However, that morning a soft breath of wind touched our faces, and God had filled the sky with bright, beautiful, and glorious sunshine. I noticed at the funeral services for Cleavon, Chaunce was being more aggressive and acted out more toward others, especially myself and Karrington. He was saying things like, "I don't want to be here," and he seemed so withdrawn and distant from everyone and everything. I knew and could tell that this was all just tearing his heart apart. Even though I tried to give him some words of comfort and encouraged him to think of all the good memories he and Cleavon had shared, even trying to get him to realize that even though Cleavon was gone to heaven, that his spirit would never leave us, and that he is even there with us right now. The next few weeks were taking a toll on my Chaunce, as well as, on me. I could feel my chest beating sometimes so fast and loud, even making me afraid to go to sleep, for fear of dying in my sleep. I just did what I could to try to console my husband, Chaunce, and my other family members. But at times, I just wanted to cry out and have someone to come and console me.

Sometimes, I just felt as if I could not please anyone. Every time when I would feel I was doing a great thing for someone else, it would come back to slap me in the face. I tried to do all I could for my children, especially, my son Chaunce, dealing with so many issues. I made so many sacrifices for him, but he did not seem to realize that, or even care. Sometimes, as I was trying to give him his medicine for his kidney care and seizures, I would call his name, and he would be absolutely so disobedient and disrespectful toward me. I would try to be patient with him, but sometimes, his behavior toward me was unbearable. I would say Chaunce, "why did you say that.?" And he would just say, I did not say anything. He would be talking out of his head to me, saying things that did not even make sense. I would have to remind myself of his brain injury, but at the same time, I would find myself breaking down crying and feeling so helpless. All I ever tried to do was to help my son, and just be there for him. The thought came to me how Chaunce had acted so awful during the Christmas holiday. I remembered that I and Karrington had gone outside for a few minutes to look around the house for one of her toys. I had left Chaunce in the house with my husband, who was upstairs taking a shave. I had spent several hours that morning wrapping Christmas gifts for our family members, not really feeling in the mood, I guess I was just not in the Christmas spirit. There were numerous gifts lying around and under the Christmas tree when we left out of the house. LORD, when I returned with Karrington from outside, I looked for some reason over to the dining room area where the tree was and started screaming. I said Chaunce what did you do? He had opened and torn apart every present under the tree that I had spent hours of time wrapping. I was just so upset and frustrated with him. I just started counting and my husband heard me I guess screaming and immediately came down stairs to see what was wrong. He thought someone was hurt. My husband was getting ready to go over to some family members' home and I just said, take Chaunce with you. I just started counting and cleaning up the mess, I wanted to just spank him, but I didn't. Again, I held it all in, my frustration I'm talking about. I even remember looking back and seeing Chaunce as he was going out of the front door, and there was a video under his arm that was one of his presents. I just sighed!!! During the holiday, I did not care to go shopping, either I was exhausted or was just not in the holiday spirit. I even remembered sitting at a drive thru service at a local restaurant, and my head was throbbing so badly, I closed my eyes, and forgot where I was I guess. I accidentally bumped the lady's car fender who was in front of me. She got out and came back to my car. I just said, miss, I so sorry, did I hurt your car. She did not see any damage and said that she was ok. That was another one of my bad days of many to come.

I remember the day we had left to go to Memphis, TN for his sleep study at Le Bonheur Children Medical Center. He had been exhibiting difficulties of sleep apnea, so the doctors there wanted him to stay overnight to conduct a sleep study. We had to arrive by 7:00 p.m. that night. I dreaded driving up the highway by myself, but my husband was out of town with his job during that time. Hesitantly, I rented a car, which we picked up at 3:00 p.m. that afternoon. My own doctor's appointment in our town had lasted longer than I thought it would and last minute errands had caused us to have to leave much later than I had planned. It was only an hour or so before dark started to fall, and I just hate driving at night. Not only that, it was raining non-stop, and with all the big, huge 18 wheelers flying by me, splashing water on my windshield, I could hardly see where I was, yet alone where I was going. Sometimes I was terrified, but I knew I had to get Chaunce to Memphis for his tests, and we did not have much time to get there. The doctors had told me that it was imperative that Chaunce stay awake after 3:00 p.m. He could not take a nap or sleep for any reason. That was a difficult task in itself. I would constantly find myself telling Chaunce, "wake up," "wake up." We only stopped a time or two at a rest stop to stretch and get some fresh air, but after Chaunce had eaten a hamburger, it was so very hard to get him to stay awake. I remembered as we continued on our journey, how the wind was blowing so hard, apparently there was a storm approaching us and it was only a few miles away. With my time quickly getting away from me, I found myself driving sometimes 80 miles an hour, in the pouring down rain, with strong winds hitting my car. Every time an 18 wheeler passed by us, and splash all that water on us, I could not see for probably a few seconds. I just found myself, PRAYING TO GOD, TO PLEASE GET US THERE SAFELY, AND TO WATCH OVER US, AND TO PLEASE GRANT US HIS MERCY. God heard every one of my prayers and never let us go. I did not want Chaunce to see the fear I had in my eyes from driving on that highway that night, but I knew that I could not stop. I could just feel my nerves shaking, and my heart feeling up with stress and anxieties. I had to keep reaching over to Chaunce to wake him up, because he wanted to sleep so badly, and was having such a hard time fighting the sleep off. I felt so bad for my son. I later stopped at the Memphis, TN state line about 7:30 p.m., and called to let them know we were almost there. This was just one of the many sacrifices I had made for my son, but I knew this was something that had to be done for him. And if I had to do it again, I know that I would be willing to do it, without giving it one thought. AND MOST OF ALL, I KNEW IT WAS ONLY BY THE GRACE OF GOD THAT WE MADE IT THERE ALIVE!!! And this is one of my many testimonies to anyone going through trials and tribulations, such as I have gone through. Just remember, that God will not leave you, nor forsake you. Remember that during those times when you think you are all alone and no one else is around and cares, remember that GOD IS THERE, HOLDING YOU UP,

BRINGING YOU THROUGH!!!

Sometimes I think to myself how sad it is that people can be so mean and cruel to someone they don't know anything about, but just that they look different. I have learned to love everyone, even those that treat you bad. I remembered the next morning as we left the hospital after having the sleep study. Chaunce and I decided to stop off at a local International House of Pancakes for breakfast. During the sleep study, the nurse had to put some thick gel on Chaunce's head in order to connect the electrolytes. I did not realize until we got there, and did not have any shampoo. We tried to wipe it out but that did not work too well. He still had white like spots in his head from the glue. As we were sitting down waiting on our food to arrive at our table, I noticed two African American women sitting over from us and starring at Chaunce, as if to say, "what's wrong with him ?." Probably wondering how could he come to eat in this place. Well, I thought to myself for a minute, I wonder should I tell them that he does not have sores in his head, and he does not have any contractual disease, and then I said, WHY SHOULD I? I don't owe them any explanation. I thought to myself, how sad it is that a person who is disabled or just looks different should have to feel out of place anywhere. If someone professes to be a Christian or a child of God, how can they allow themselves to feel or even think this way. I just looked back at them and smiled, and continued my conversation with Chaunce. I did say a prayer for them for God to heal their spirit, and to cleanse their soul. Later on that day, we made it back to Jackson to pick up Karrington from my mother's and then attempted to drive on home to Terry, which was about 25-30 miles further down the highway. I was so very exhausted driving up and from Memphis, and having only a few hours of sleep at the hospital. I thought about some of Chaunce's medicine being out, and said "Oh, no", I have to stop by the pharmacy too. By the time I picked up his medicine, and got back on the highway heading home, I was so tired, and exhausted I could hardly speak. I just remember praying to God, and asking him to Lord, please grant me your mercy, and drive me home. I knew that if anyone knew God definitely knew how stressed and drained my body was. God did drive me home, because I know I certainly did not. HE IS MY ROCK, AND FOREVER MY SALVATION. LORD, THANK YOU!!! LORD, THANK YOU!!!

Having gone through so many sacrifices, such as this, was one reason I was so upset one day while driving home, Chaunce made the statement, that "I did not love him." I felt so hurt, knowing all the struggles and trials I had been through with him, and never once putting myself ahead of him, no matter what the cost. I just told him, Chaunce, if I didn't love you, would I do all the things I do for you to keep you well. Making sure you always have what you needed. Baby, if I did not love you, I wouldn't worry about you when you get sick, and stay in hospital after hospital for countless nights just to make sure you got the medical attention you needed. You should know that I love you. That to me just felt like a kick in my stomach. I thought about how I got up morning after morning getting him and Karrington ready for school, struggling day after day with his defiant behavior making every attempt to keep my sanity. How he would purposefully be disobedient sometimes seeming like it was just to upset me, and constantly hurt my heart. I also recalled, how we would start almost every morning off when he was small, before his kidney transplant, with him throwing up as soon as I placed him in his car seat, and having to go back in the house and change his clothes, clean him up, all this before I even started my day teaching my class. I would so many days get to work, feeling as if I had already done a full days work, feeling so overwhelmed. The memories also flashed across my mind how when I was eight months pregnant with Karrington, I was taking him back and forth to Memphis for his kidney checkups, once a week, once a month, and later every two months. Remembering running and walking fast through the airport, holding his hand, with three bags or more in the other hand trying to get to my rental car, sometimes having to switch cars up in the rain, and hardly being able to move my body around. I just recalled going through so much, and I knew it was for my Chaunce's best interest, for his well- being, and nothing else mattered. I always felt as if I could do more for my children. I seemed to always feel I was inadequate as a parent, and as a mother.

Then, the next week, as we were dealing with so much death and pain in our family during the Christmas holiday, my oldest daughter caused me to break down into tears. She had asked me to get her a p-coat for Christmas. I did not really know what that was. I went to the mall walking up and down the aisles, from store to store looking, but many stores did not have them, or one in her size, or even one she would like. She had asked me to go to a particular store, which had one that she liked. I went to that store, and I could not get any help from the sales lady, they were so busy. So, I looked around myself, and did not see any more p-coats. I went down to a very nice store, and got a p-coat, which I thought was great. I even asked the salesperson, if this was something that a young lady would like, she quickly answered, "I don't see why they would not like it, I wish someone would buy me one those coats." It was a very, very, nice Ann-Cline coat with very nice details. The p-coat ended up costing me almost $200.00, and that did not include the very nice giftwrap, which I waited to be done before I had left the mall. I wanted to surprise Tiffiani, so I left it under the Christmas tree at my mother's house, where she was staying. Strangely enough, on Christmas morning, Tiffani opened the box and called me immediately, I thought to thank me for the coat. I could not understand what she was saying, only that she was screaming to the top of her lungs in my ear. She was saying, "Mom, why did you buy this awful coat, and I just know you could not have thought I would like it." "Why didn't you do what I asked you to do?" I told her that I did go to that store, but they did not have anymore. She just called me lazy for not looking harder to find her what she wanted, and that I only think about myself and no one else. I hung up the telephone and burst into tears. Saying to myself, "why can't I do anything right?" Why can't I please my children?" With all the stress and turmoil going on in our family this experience made me feel that much more down in my spirits and depressed. I did not want to go anywhere that entire Christmas Day.

It was not the first time Tiffani was so very mean and rude to me. Despite all that I have tried to do for her, it just seemed as is she was ashamed of me for some reason. I quickly remembered how hurt I was when Tiffani was preparing to board a bus for her senior trip to Florida. I had been running all around town getting things she needed and doing whatever she needed me to do. When we got to the school all the parents were standing around talking with other parents and to other students. Tiffani didn't seem to want me to talk much to anyone. After spending a large sum of money for her expenses here getting ready for the trip, the Lord had blessed me to give her

$300.00 for spending money. I thought this was a good amount, but when I gave it to her, she so rudely made the comment, "Is this all?" I held my feelings back in shock for what she said. She did not want me to even board the bus to tell her goodbye and to give her a hug. She kept saying, "mom, get off the bus, get off the bus." As I was leaving the bus the other parents were coming on and they had decided we needed to say a prayer with the kids before the bus departed. I felt so bad, and my self- esteem was knocked down so low, as if I had been kicked in my stomach. However, I had come to accept that nothing I would do for Tiffani would ever be enough.

But later I realized that it was not just my children who were stressing me out, but also my husband. I had gotten my husband something for Christmas, one of which was two packs of boxer shorts and t-shirts. When he saw the boxers, he immediately said to me, "why did you get me a large, I could have worn a medium size?" I thought I had done right since I was going by the measurement sizes on the package. After minutes of hearing negative comments from him, I just said "ok", and left out of the kitchen in tears. He did not realize that earlier that day, I had gone through so much stress at work, when one of my coworkers became seriously sick, and could not breathe correctly, it had been a horrible, frightful day, not knowing if she would make it or not. We were there rushing around trying to get her family members on the phone and calling emergency personnel. I could feel my nerves that night just coming unglued. I was just screaming inside my body, but no sounds were coming out, and no one was listening to me. I guess this and the incident at work, and being just days from when Tiffani had verbally attacked me, my nerves just could not take anymore. I later found myself sitting in the corner of the sitting room in the dark, just crying, and crying and crying. My nerves were crumbling, and I just began to talk to God. He knew what I was going through and that was when I knew everything else around me did not matter. When I exchanged my husband's boxers the next day, it turned out that the size I had gotten was right. The size he wanted was too small. I carried them back to the store to exchange them again, returned and gave them to him. I did not say "I told you so", or "I knew I was right." As I looked into my husband's eyes, I felt like he was expecting me to say that, but I didn't. God had taken care of my pain and taught me that he will always fight my battles. God had taught me better. His guilty conscious was payback enough for me.

My body seemed to be so tired and exhausted and no matter how much I did for Chaunce or my family, in my husband's eyes it was to me always not enough. I felt that he did not understand the amount of stress I dealt with on a daily basis. My goodness, he was hardly ever around when I was to me like running a marathon trying to keep up with what all I had to do. I would move so fast doing five or six things at a time and not even realizing the impact it had on my body. I would clean the house, feed the children, give Chaunce his medicine, and treatments, get the children bathed and dressed, with sometimes having to plead with Chaunce to get out of the tub, only to be faced with defiance and awful behavior. When he would sometimes come home from his job, driving across country, or he would take a nap after his trip, he would awake just as I sat down to finally breathe. He would come through the room where I was sitting and think I was sitting there all morning. He would give me that look or make a sound and I just knew what he was thinking. Sometimes I would wonder what would happen if something were to happen to me. Who would take care of the children, feed them, see about getting their homework done, which he never would offer to help do unless I asked for his help. I would always tell my husband that he needed to learn how to give Chaunce his medicine, in case I was not around to do so. This seemed to go in one ear and out the other. My physician who I was seeing at the time suggested one day after my annual checkup, that I seek the attention of a psychiatrist. She could tell that I truly needed some emotional counseling. When I went in to see this psychiatrist, he noted that I had mentioned the word RESENTMENT toward my husband at least four times during our first two-hour session.

I recalled how Chaunce would torment Karrington sometimes nonstop on our way home. I could not leave him alone with her even for a minute, especially in the car. I remember how I would get out to pump gas, and the short amount of time I would be outside the car, he would call her horrible names, which of course, he would deny when asked, would reach from the back seat and punch her in the shoulder or worst, I just seem to have no where to turn. I would be stressed out all the way home day in and day out. My mother and my sister

Dorothy, as well as, a few of my husband's family members, were the only ones I could ask to watch Chaunce for a short while to give me a break. Everyone else seemed to either be too busy or would have a thousand excuses for not being able to help. I think it was a lot of the times, due to his disruptive, and impulsive behavior. Sometimes, I would find myself crying while I was driving down the road, barely seeing where I was going. I began to realize that my family was dysfunctional, at least in my eyes, and very special. As time went on, my husband began to become more helpful with the children.

That night before I went to bed, I was remembering the time we went to Memphis for Chaunce's checkup for his kidney. We thought it was a regular visit; however, after having Chaunce's blood drawn, the doctors wanted us to have him admitted to the hospital, due to abnormal levels of his liver count which was very serious. We did not come prepared to stay, and we also did not seem to have a choice in the matter. I frowned at the thought of spending the night, especially with having Karrington along with us. That I knew was going to be added stress, and my husband I could tell was beginning to feel some of the stress I had felt all these years. In fact, he had even began taking care of Chaunce more, especially during the night, such as getting him up to use the bathroom, and giving him water to drink. He was very concerned about Chaunce's kidney condition. The kids were becoming restless, and we did not have a chance to get lunch until much later in the evening. We were confronted with talking to numerous doctors, sitting in waiting rooms for countless hours, and having our anxiety levels raised a mile a minute. Chaunce and Karrington were becoming very disruptive because they had not eaten for several hours. We were finally able to grab a bite to eat. I remembered being in the Emergency Room trying to get Chaunce admitted still having to wait. They were still running countless tests on his blood to check his liver counts. My husband had gone to park the car and had taken Karrington with him. After I had come to an examination room with Chaunce, I just happened to look in the Emergency room next door, and my husband John had let the admissions staff admit Karrington who of course was not there to be seen. My poor little girl was so exhausted and I remembered how she was walking holding my husband's hand with her head hanging back, and I just said, "my poor baby." Well, I can say this did give us a good laugh, which helped to relieve some of our stress. We finally got to a bedroom about 2 a.m. that morning.

One morning, which was on a Friday, as I was getting ready for work, I had taken my bath and as I was preparing to get dressed I took a look in the mirror, just looking at my image and my Lord God delivered me and I got the holy ghost. The Lord began to reveal to me why all the things bad and good had happened in my life. I just remembered I began hopping up and down, screaming Thank you Lord, Thank you God, just praising him and giving him all the glory. I recalled I started crying and crying and just could not stop. I guess I was having so many flashbacks of all the pain and suffering I had endured for so many years. It didn't even occur to me that I wasn't even dressed yet, it really didn't matter, I just continued to cry, praise and thank God for showing me why I had suffered so many heartaches, pain and misery, and most of all why my son Chaunce had gone through all the pain, after pain, after tragedy throughout his entire life. I was throwing my hands up in the air, and I remembered thinking to myself it felt like fire shut up in my bones, I had always heard this expression at church services, but never had the opportunity to actually feel what it meant, and that was truly what it felt like, "fire shut up in my bones." I was realizing that all these years of pain was not due to anything I was causing or Chaunce was causing, but that it was all God's will, God's plan for our lives. After I got dressed, I came into the kitchen and continued feeling so overwhelmed with all the things the Lord was beginning to reveal to me. He was showing me that the pain I suffered at my jobs and the agony I had gone through with the awful people in my life was never in my control. It was not what I did, it had nothing to do with me. God was revealing to me that he had written my script, which was MY LIFE. He was showing me that he wanted me to tell this story to people in hopes of maybe inspiring them and allowing them to know and realize that there was light at the end of the dark, dark, tunnel, just like it was for me, it was like he was saying, "look at your life Rita, don't you see now that I never left you, I was always there holding your hand." I began to realize at that moment that God had prepared a book for me to write, the script that would hopefully help so many people, and impact their lives, "IT WAS MY LIFE."

I just felt so overjoyed and just could not stop thanking Jesus, I remembered, I kept saying, "Thank you Lord, Thank you Lord." I was running around the kitchen, crying, and screaming with joy. The Lord just kept on revealing to me different stages of my life and showing me that this was why this happen, this was why that happened. He was letting me see that if I had not been tormented and guided to do this, I would not have received the blessing that I did. I could not for the life of me understand at that time why things were going so bad in my life. It seemed as if the more I tried to distance myself from trouble and mess at work, the more I was caught in the middle of mess…mess that I had no control over. I couldn't understand why I was dealing with so much stress and tribulations. I always tried to do what I could for my family and what I thought was right, but for some reason, that did not matter. Somehow, it would always turn out for the worst for me. God was letting me see how if I were not pushed into this corner, I would not have received this blessing and that blessing. I just remember how I started holding my chest and taking deep breaths. IT WAS SO AWESOME!!! However, I remembered that we serve an AWESOME GOD!!!

I was finally able to calm down enough to get the kids up and get them ready for school. I was so excited, but I did not want to scare them by screaming any more, so I tried to contain my blessing, my wonderful revelation. On my way to work, I just started to think back about Chaunce's life and I just broke down on my steering wheel crying. When I got to work, I was so excited I just wanted to shout and tell the whole world what I had come to know, and how I felt, but the Lord showed me the time was not right. It took so much for me to contain myself all that day. I remembered I left work that day and went over to my school where I had recently transferred from, I had been at that school for over four years and had formed a strong bond with the co-workers in my department. The teachers there, I felt would be there for me and could understand more about what I was experiencing because they had been there through so many of my stressful and painful years, they knew how I and my family had been suffering. When I came in they immediately could tell that something was just not right, they knew that I was not myself. I guess I was so overjoyed they could tell something was wrong, but did not know what to think. One of the teachers, I recalled, ran and got me some water, they were beginning to think that I was hyperventilating. I began to tell them about my morning experience, and how God had shown me his plans for my family. I was trying to tell them, but I guess I was so excited, that I could hardly get it out that God had revealed to me his plans for me to write a book. I said YES! I am going to write a book. The script I told them was already thought out, and that God had written the script for me, and that it was my life, my children's life, my family's life. I told them that I would plan a party, a party with a purpose, which would be to announce that I was going to write a book. I knew that God wanted this book to be written in order to help so many people. I told them that this book was going to help people that read it who maybe had been suffering pain, trials, and tribulations as we had gone through for so many years, and that it might perhaps give them hope and inspiration and help them to realize that the trials we go through and suffer is not always our will, but God's will. That God has a plan for all of us and that he would never leave us nor forsake us, no matter how much it may seem to be sometimes. I knew for myself that God also wanted me to help the homeless people I passed everyday coming in and going out of town. It seemed to me like he had mapped my pathway just so that I would pass several of the homeless shelters in our downtown urban location. There was a reason. I knew that he wanted me to see that there were other people suffering and needing help. He put me in that situation because he wanted me to be one of the ones to offer help, and to offer hope.

I remembered the day we had prepared to leave church. Our pastor mentioned that it had been a wonderful holiday season for probably most of us. He stated that we should be thankful for what we have and share our blessings with those who are less fortunate. I did as my pastor asked. Upon completing Christmas dinner, I prepared food to be taken to someone in town whom I felt would be blessed of it. I passed several people, but I knew the Lord would show me that person he knew truly needed my help. I drove down the main street in downtown Jackson and came pass a man whom was homeless. He saw that I had slowed down and he came over toward my truck. He stated that he had not eaten much all that day and had recently gotten out of jail after being arrested for sleeping in an abandoned building. He was so thankful and appreciative for what I gave him. I asked him if he had somewhere to sleep that night, and he said, no miss, I really don't. I mentioned the homeless shelter I had passed on my way into town, but he said that they charged $5.00 to get in. I did not have much change on me, but I gave him $20.00 that I did have. I realized that GOD has blessed me in order to share what I have with those in need. I had such a wonderful feeling blessing someone else and for a few moments forgetting the ordeal and problems I was enduring. God was showing me just how blessed I truly was, despite the pain and suffering my family was going through.

A few days later as I was driving home to Terry, I stopped to get some coffee at a local convenience store. As I was in line paying for my coffee I noticed the clerk was speaking to an elderly man who was paying for his gas. Apparently, he only gave her 3 cents, yes… I said 3 pennies. I remembered the clerk told him, sir, this won't get you much gas at all, and the man replied, that's all I have. The man had turned and had begun to walk out of the door. I just thought to myself, I couldn't possibly let him try to get home with this and not try to help him. I told the clerk that I wanted to pay $10.00 for his gas, and she stated to me, you are going to be so blessed. I just said to her, mam, I am already so blessed!! All of God's goodness and mercy began to flash across my mind. I said to myself, "God, you are so good to me. As the man walked out of the door, he looked back at me and whispered, thank you. So despite what trials and tribulations my family and I had been enduring, we must remember to praise God for his glory. That is what the bible means, when we read, "We must remember to praise God inspite of our circumstances!!!

That night when I got home, I had my daughter and her best friend over to the house, so I could tell them what had happened to me that day. I sat my daughter and her friend, my goddaughter, as I call her, down and began to explain to them what had happened that morning. It had to be around 12:00 that night and we were sitting there talking, I was not tired, I seemed to have so much energy. My daughter knew I had some news, but she did not know exactly what the news was. She was so anxious, that she could not wait for me to explain to her how God had changed my life for the better. Her friend kept saying to her, "Tiffani, just hush and wait, let your mother tell us what happened" in her own way, but Tiffani continued to be impatient. I began telling them how God had revealed to me that morning how all the pain, turmoil, and suffering all my family and I had endured was for a reason. I told them how God had shown me his plans for me to write a book. I told them that the script was already written, it was My Life, and that God had ordered my steps for a reason. I was so excited I went on talking and talking and talking. I couldn't even eat much of anything that day. I just had no appetite. After talking for over an hour, Tiffani and her friend decided to spend the night. They went on to bed, but I could not sleep. I guess I was still too excited. I sat up and talked to God and read my Bible most of that night. I was drawn to a certain verse in the Bible, and I kept coming back to it. It was the Book of Isiah-Chapter 25:1, and it read, "O'Lord, you are my God, I will exalt you and praise your name for in perfect faithfulness God you have done marvelous things, things planned long ago."

I finally fell off asleep for a few hours and got up. I remembered how I went into the bathroom and all of a sudden, I threw up. I thought it was strange, because I knew that I had hardly eaten anything to be throwing up. I just thought it was because I was so excited. I recalled that when I threw up, it was something with an orange color. I thought it was very strange, because I had not eaten anything of that color, and I just could not think what it could possibly be. My daughter woke up and found me sitting at the dining room table. She quietly asked me, "Mom, have you been to bed at all?" I told her yes, but she could still see that I was very excited. I was finding myself thinking back to when I was in the store the night before, and I saw a close friend whom I had not seen in a while. It seemed like the entire incident of seeing her was occurring in slow motion. Almost as if I was not in control of my actions, not even my own body. After starring at me for some time that morning, Tiffani was under the impression that I might be suffering a nervous breakdown, or what she called "bipolar disorder." I assured her that I was fine and just excited about how God had shown me the reasons for so many of my pain and heartaches. By that time, I had begun to feel tired and somewhat exhausted. But, I still seem to have a spiritual high where I was so full of energy. I felt like people say you feel when you are excited about the Lord. It felt like "fire shut up in my bones." I guess I just could not hold it in. I just could not keep God's goodness to myself. I had to go to choir rehearsal at my church that morning around 11:00 a.m., so I told Tiffani to take the children, Chaunce and Karrington, with her to eat breakfast and I would meet them at the restaurant before I headed to church. I remembered when I got there I was still so excited, and bursting over with joy and just happy. I remembered so many times when I didn't know what it felt like to be happy, and now the Lord had blessed me to feel somewhat at peace. Tiffani kept saying, "Mom, calm down, you're beginning to scare me." I told her I was fine and that I was in God's hands. As I sat down to order our breakfast, I saw Chaunce's teacher from the Rehabilitation Center where he was at for several weeks after he suffered his traumatic brain injury. She was the one who began teaching him academics at the Center. I thought this was truly a sign from God, because it was such a coincidence that we both would be there at that time. I knew that God was once again ordering my steps having us to be at that place at the same time. I went over to her and began telling her how Chaunce was doing and how much he had improved since leaving the Rehabilitation Center. She could not believe how much he had grown. I then began telling her of my plans, no, I mean God's plan for me to write a book of my life, of my testimonies. I shared with her how the Lord had shown to me his plans for me to help others through this book. She thought it was a great idea, and said she really wanted to read it when it was completed. I also spoke to a lady who was in a wheelchair, trying to order her breakfast, but could not see the wall menu for the countertop. I offered to order her breakfast for her after she told me what she wanted. I told her that I taught special needs children and was looking toward writing a book, which would allow me to help disabled persons and support various organizations. She was also truly excited and I told her that I just felt from my experiences of having a special needs child myself, I realized that often our loved ones are looked over and not always given the assistance they need. I said to her that I really wanted to change that. God was showing me his visions and his purpose for writing this book.

I guess I felt so overwhelmed because I was so overjoyed finally knowing that my son's suffering was for a reason. I thought back about his kidney condition he had always suffered, the medications he had to endure taking, the near fatal drowning, the traumatic brain injury, the seizures, the sleep apnea, and all the pain and suffering. I always thought to myself, this is just too much pain for anyone person to suffer, especially a small child. Just to know that all along God had this planned…a miracle in the making. I thought back in my mind how some people would tell me that God would never leave you, nor forsake you, and now I realized that all this time he was always there, holding my hand, picking me up, and giving me the energy to stand, when all I wanted to do was to fall down and give up!! I just could not help but to keep telling God, "Thank You, Thank You." She just did not realize how much her mother had been through. I don't think anyone really knew, except GOD!!!! My daughter, Tiffani still had difficulty realizing why I was so overjoyed, she just kept insisting that I was losing my mind. I recalled what my pastor had said one night at bible class, about people sometimes not being able to understand your praise. That when they see you run down an aisle or jump up for joy thanking God, even though it may seem strangely, peculiar to them, we know, I KNEW what I was thanking God for, it didn't matter what other people, especially Tiffani thought. I just told her that I was fine, GOD HAS ME, I AM FINALLY OK. Still, in this joyous mood I remembered ordering this big breakfast for the kids and myself, and I did not even take a bite of it. I was already feeling so full, that I was just not hungry. I left the restaurant a little sooner than they did trying to get to my church rehearsal, and asked Tiffani to take the kids to my mom's house. I could tell she was still worried about me, and I told her I was ok to drive. The next few days were like I was living a dream, and part of which I don't even remember.

When I got to church, the choir was already in the choir stand and the moment I came in I immediately started feeling the Holy Spirit. I was so happy I just couldn't contain myself. As I said earlier, it felt like fire shut up in my bones. Before I knew it, I started running up and down the aisles of the church and told the members of the choir I had some wonderful news to share with them. I then spoke with the first lady of the church and a wonderful friend, who through all of my trials and tribulations was always there to encourage me and consistently sent me little notes and greeting cards to inspire me. At first they thought I had gotten the calling to minister, and I told them not quite. I did not realize until later that they had called our pastor to come and see about me. I remembered coming back into the sanctuary and holding my hands up praising the Lord, and walking up and down the aisles. I told the choir, whom by this time had stopped singing and was probably trying to figure out what in heavens name was wrong with me. They knew that this was totally out of my character. I then said to them, I am going to write a book you all. The Lord has given me a book to write, and he has shown me how it is going to help to get our church built. For many months the church had been planning to build a new church, because the congregation had grown so much in size that the church could not hold everyone. But raising the funds to build it was not an easy task. I told the church members, the Lord is blessing us, he is blessing us right now. Oh Lord, thank you; thank you. I began to cry and jump up and down and cry and cry and suddenly found myself stretched out on the floor in the middle aisle. Everyone was looking and then members started to come to me to help me up and fan me, rubbing my forehead, and saying it's going to be alright. They probably still just did not realize how the Lord was blessing me in the spirit.

When I laid down in the middle aisle on my back, I could just think about how good God was to me. I felt so happy, if only for a short time, happier than I had felt in such a long time. My church members did not know what exactly to think. They were trying to console me and calm me down. Shortly, after that the pastor came in. I told the members I was fine and just wanted to talk to the pastor. The pastor was excited about my news, but he said he wanted me to be around to enjoy my blessing and my children. So, I calmed down and began telling him how God had begun to reveal to me why things happened in my life all these years, how all the pain and suffering I had endured, and the struggles were meant for a reason, and how he had been ordering my steps in order to complete this journey.

He could tell just by talking with me that I had suffered so much pain, as well as, my son and our family. He could feel all this hurt in my heart, and could see that I was now being shown the reason behind all of it. I told him that I was calm now, but he insisted that someone drive me to my mother's home, he said that he did not want me to drive. My church members, I just love them so, were so concerned about my well-being, in fact, one of the choir members took my keys and said she would drive me to my mother's. She said that she did not want me to hurt myself or maybe worse. By this time when I got to my mom's home, I was still so energized but realized that I had to calm down and take care of my family, as well as, myself. But when I got to my mother's I called one of my sisters, and told her I had such wonderful news and I wanted to share it with our entire family. So that evening I was able to get most of my close relatives to meet me at my oldest sister's home.

We sat in a circle in which I was in a chair in the center. I began to tell my family what things were going on with me and how the Lord God was revealing wonderful things to me concerning my future, our family's future, and showing me how, and why certain things, and occurrences had taken place in my life, and especially in my children's lives. As I began to talk and witness to them, some of my family members, particularly my sister, Bernice, and my niece, Angela, as well as, my cousin in-law, Nancy, whom were very much anointed in the spirit, could tell, that God was indeed using me, and also see that the devil was trying to enter my mind and spirit in order to destroy God's wonderful blessings he had in store for my family. My sister told me that God had chosen me to take care of Chaunce. God knew that Chaunce's life would be one of trials and tremendous tribulations, and that it would take a very special person to endure the stress and agony, which was to lie ahead. She said that, "God had chosen me to give birth to Chaunce and take care of him through all his illnesses while he was here on this earth. Going through all Chaunce had been going through was God's plan to use our experience in order to help other people, going through similar or even worse situations, helping them through our testimonies and words of hope and faith. They were letting me know that God's plan was for me to help many people. As in the bible it says, "That I may publish with the voice of thanksgiving, and tell of all thy wondrous works." Matthew 26:7

We talked about how I mentioned about me throwing up that night after God began revealing to me of his blessings and why certain experiences had occurred in my life. I was told that I was slain in the spirit, and I was actually letting God in through my heart and soul. The devil was trying to discern the spirit. He did not want me to receive God's gifts. My sister and niece were talking about how a person reacts when they are in the Holy Spirit, and it was strange as I was listening to them, because what they were saying was exactly what was happening with me. They mentioned how the person will be running and just fall out in the spirit, and how they will purge something that is orange in color. They also mentioned a verse in the bible, and my God, I told them that it was the exact same verse I had read that night while I sat in bed before I purged that next morning, and had read it just before they arrived at my sister Rosie's house. I ran and got my bible and showed it to them. I just could not believe what was happening. That experience was so AWESOME!!!!! The verse I remembered was from the book of Isaiah Chapter 25:1 and it read "O Lord, you are my God. I will exalt you and praise your name for in perfect faithfulness God you have done marvelous things, things planned long ago."

After a while, my family all began talking how God was in fact using me and the devil was after my soul. They wanted to protect me from the devil so they decided that I did not need to go home alone since my husband John was out of town. They had me to lie on the floor, as the Holy Spirit began to take over my body. I was not myself it seemed to me. They decided to call an ambulance and have me to stay at the hospital over night where I would be safer. When they tried to protect me and exercise the devil out of my spirit, who probably because of all God's goodness he had in store for me, was trying to take over my body. I guess the devil was trying to turn something wonderful and good from the Lord into something bad and evil, but I was not going to let that happen, and neither was my family. As they were holding my body down on the floor until the ambulance arrived, they told me to let them know if I was all right. They did not want to hurt me. Sometimes, I could not tell if it was my family members or the devil pretending to be them. The demon devil was all around the room, trying to undo all the good and marvelous work the Lord had done, especially as he was showing us what was about to happen. When the ambulance got there, they did not understand what was happening. They thought I was trying to attack my family members and that the family was restraining me for that. Both of the paramedics were wrong, my family loved me and I loved them. I knew that they were trying to protect me. We had to devise a secret code for me to let them know that I was all right and that God was over my spirit now and in CONTROL. I told them if I said, "He's revealing it to me," they should know that I was not talking out of my head, and that God was only revealing to me different stages of my life, showing me the pain I and my family had endured, and revealing to me why it had happened. God was showing us that through all the bad and horrible things we had been through, it was his plan to use those experiences to help someone else. He was revealing to me all the wonderful blessings he had in store for us. God was showing me how he wanted me to use this book to help the homeless and others who could not help themselves, and how he wanted me to use proceeds from this book to help inspire the lives of so many people.

When I got in the ambulance, the paramedics began to restrain me and ask me all sorts of questions. They could tell by my answers that I was in fact in my right mind. One of them even commented that I knew quite a bit to be ill. My blood pressure was also very good they said. When I arrived at the hospital some of my family members were there to meet me. They were so concerned about me. If I said, "He's revealing it to me," they knew that I was ok. That was our secret code you see. The nurse began asking me several questions and taking my vital signs. I remembered that Tiffani's best friend, Brangelia, was sitting near my bed and my nephew was also there. Brangelia had always been there for Tiffani, even when I could not be, and I was indebted to her, and she was truly a blessing. The next thing I remembered is that the nurse gave me a sedative and I must have passed out right away.

When I awoke, it was so strange to me. I remembered hearing the speaker system in the hospital announce that breakfast would be served shortly, and I recalled saying, "When did they start serving breakfast in the Emergency Room?" I thought I was still in the Emergency Room on that same Saturday night I was brought in by the paramedics, but to my surprise, I was in fact in a patient room, and several days had passed. I did not even realize it. My sister later told me that they walked down the hallway beside me on the way to my room and I did not even remember any of it. I ended up staying in the hospital for two weeks, and the first week was a complete blank to me. I saw a newspaper, and read that things had happened for days of which I had absolutely no account. In the process of receiving God's wonderful blessings and revelations my body had become so exhausted and I guess I just couldn't handle it anymore. My family members were able to care for Chaunce and give him all of his medications as he needed. This was something that never happened, since the day Chaunce was born. I mean, I had never been separated from Chaunce since his birth, between giving him his medications, and performing dialysis on him, I never had the opportunity to just sleep through the entire night. My family was concerned about me, and insisted that I rest and take care of myself. This seemed so strange, because for so many years, I had never thought about taking care of myself. Everyone else's well-being always seemed to take priority over me. God was showing me that it was time for me to rest, or to exhale, as I sometimes think of it. My daughter had continued to think that I was having a nervous breakdown or suffering from some bipolar disorder. But they just did not know and couldn't know or understand how wonderful it felt when God began to give me sweet rest, sweet wonderful rest, something that I had needed for so many years, for so long. They did not understand the life my children, Karrington and Chaunce, as well as, myself, were living. To me it was worse than being dysfunctional, it was more like being trapped in a cave for years, with no where to turn and no way to get out, with no one knowing how or when to come to your survival. But God was showing me that he was in control, not me. I was so thankful, I could not help but to continue praising God!! The doctors were beginning to think that I was suffering a breakdown, or was completely stressed out, which part of that was true. I was in fact completely stressed, but even they could not understand what all I had been through these past years, and the amazing experience I was witnessing. My daughter, Tiffani and my husband just wanted me to do whatever the doctors said, so I could get well and come home. They kept saying, "stop talking out of your head, you are sounding so crazy. God is not talking to you, and don't you tell anyone that he is."

They just did not know that I had developed a special relationship with God, and it felt SO WONDERFUL, SO WONDERFUL!!! I had come to realize that God was always there for me, even when I did not think he was, and he had never left me.

During the next week, I spent all my energy trying to convince the doctors that I was in fact, all right. I was confined to one hospital floor, on which I could not leave for any reason. I did not see the outside for the entire time I was there. I even had to get permission to use the telephone or have visitors. The doctors kept insisting that I take this strong medication, and I was beginning to refuse it because every time I would take the medicine, it seemed as if I would be unconscious for hours and hours, and I did not want that to happen. I recalled the day I kept asking when I was going to be allowed to leave, but I could never get a straight answer from anyone. I was taken to a room when I refused to take the strong dose of medicine. It was a room at the end of a long hallway, where security guards removed my glasses, and my tennis shoes. I kept asking them, "What are you going to do?" They never would say. They held me and restrained me while someone from the medical staff gave me a shot in my arm. I kept saying to them, "I don't need any more medicine, I don't want any more medicine, and why are you doing this to me?" I just wanted to know why they were hurting me. After that, I remembered being taken back to my room and I could barely walk, and within a matter of less than a few minutes, I was passed out again. I don't even remember how long. I was beginning to lose track of time, and losing track of days. I was allowed to visit with my husband and daughter, as well as, my pastor and two of my church members. During the next few days I continued to talk to God while I was alone in my room. I did not want others to hear me for fear of what might happen to me. I asked God to please continue to show me and guide me in what he would have me to do. I kept saying, "God, whatever is your will." The end of the second week, I was finally allowed to leave. In order for this to happen though I had to begin agreeing with the doctors, my daughter, and my husband. They only listened to the doctors not at all to me. I told them that I would take the medicines the doctors had prescribed, but I knew that I had no intentions of continuing to put that evil medication in my body. I knew there was nothing wrong with me, even if they didn't. My spirits continued to be so high, but my husband and daughter refused to hear what I was saying. My husband, in fact, even said to me, "If you go to work talking that crazy stuff the people at your job are going to let you go, they are going to think that you have lost your mind." I just stopped in my tracks and thought to myself, if after all these years, and what I have been through, I have not lost my mind yet, why would he think that I would lose it now. But then, I remembered, and said to myself, "He never truly realized what I was going through." "He never experienced my suffering, and pain, as well as, what our two children had gone through.

My life seemed to be going over one hurdle after another. It seemed as if before I would come out of one storm, I was already in another one. Shortly, after that incident, my husband began feeling ill as if he had a chest cold or bronchitis. He went to the doctor thinking to himself that he would be given medication to cure a common chest cold. Unfortunately, his doctor told him that he seriously had something much more than a cold. He asked the doctors should he take off work to have more tests done. They told him he would have to be off for way more than a few days. Their diagnosis was that he had two, maybe three blocked arteries and needed to have immediate heart bypass surgery. He was stunned, as I was when he got home and shared this news with me. I just thought back to myself of my tests I had gone through with my mammogram, and just said, "Lord, no." All I knew at that point is was to leave it in the Lord's hands. I immediately asked him if he would seek a second opinion and he said they told him he was welcome to seek a second opinion, but that time was of the essence. They did not want him to risk having a heart attack, which is what would have happened if he put surgery off for too long. They told him that having a heart attack would definitely only make matters much worse. When things like this happen in your life, you often think, "why me?" What I thought was that it could have been much worse. What if he had been out on his job, driving across country to Texas, and had had a heart attack, with no one around, and no place to go? I told my husband, we should be so thankful to God for showing us this at that time, when he was home, and could get help. I told him that God was already working it out, and that we should just know for ourselves that he is in control, and everything would be all right. In fact, I knew God was already working it out, because he made it happen that one of my husband's church members came by his hospital room, and talked with him. He had already had a triple heart bypass and God had brought him through. He told my husband about his experience, and it seemed to calm my husband's nerves a bit. We must remember that it is not up to us to question God's will, and so many times people do not seem to realize or acknowledge that. We prayed and asked God to lead and guide us, because I knew that no one else but God could work it out and lead us through this storm. My husband had never before had surgery but was now about to prepare for a very, very risky surgery, that could mean life or death for him. During the next week he had several tests done to prepare him for surgery. The day of my husband's surgery I had never before seen him more nervous but despite his abundance of anxieties, he knew that God was there and would be holding his hand during the entire ordeal. His family members, friends, church members, and co-workers were all there to offer moral support and strength. I could tell that day of surgery while we were in the holding area, that he was very on edge, and knew this was not good for his blood pressure. I just told him to pray to God to work it out, and he would. **HE DID!!!** Just before going back for his surgery, the doctors confirmed it to us that he did in fact, based on test results, have three blocked arteries. That we knew it meant he would be having a triple heart bypass. I just recalled saying, "OH LORD, HELP US!!! GOD, PLEASE KEEP US IN YOUR CARE."

The next day after surgery and in fact the entire week, I never had seen my husband in such a vulnerable state. He was totally dependent on others for assistance, which is something my husband never before would allow to happen. I remember when I looked back on those times when I was down and unable to fulfill my wifely obligations, and now God had allowed him to be in my shoes. His pride did not stand in the way of letting me help him. He knew I was there for him, no matter what. I took my vows very seriously when I said to him, "in sickness and in health, for better or worse." I think to myself sometimes, HOW GOD SOMETIMES HAVE TO BREAK US DOWN IN ORDER FOR US TO BECOME MORE HUMBLE, MORE GRATEFUL, AND MORE THANKFUL. It's a reminder that we should always give praise, and glory to him, OUR ALMIGHTY. I also knew that if I made this pledge to my husband, I was also making this pledge to My God, and I have always had every intention of keeping it. Because open- heart surgery is so serious and life threatening, he was not able or allowed to do much of anything. I remembered helping him to get to the bathroom. Helping to bathe him and get him dressed, even feed him. Whatever my husband needed, I would be there for him and I just prayed he would realize through all this just how much I truly loved him. I also hoped that he would realize that a husband and wife sometimes have to go through trials and tribulations together, if they expect to weather the storms in the future, they can't do it apart from one another. Hopefully, this experience will make us stronger as individuals and more understanding and compassionate as soul mates. Now, we truly appreciate the care and concern we have for each other.

During the next few months we continued to struggle with getting Chaunce the medical care he needed. He continued to have seizure episodes. One day, he had a bad seizure at school and fell down to the floor. His teachers were very frightened and concerned for him. They called me at work frantic about his safety, and I immediately rushed over to his school to get him. Chaunce had always had such caring and concerned teachers while he was in school. They seemed to be compassionate and had empathy for him. But this year, he was in a school where his teacher was truly an angel sent from God. I felt that way because of how she always had patience and took time with him. Despite his disability and learning difficulties, she worked with him so well and encouraged him to see all the potential he had. She seemed to always have such a spiritual bond with her students and I truly appreciated and admired that. Sister Daniels was to me such a rare person, both as an individual and as a teacher. She seemed to have qualities only someone could get from our Lord, Jesus.

As time went on and Chaunce's seizures began to get worse, along with his sleep apnea, I awoke many a nights sometimes before day in the morning to find Chaunce shaking and going through an awful seizure spell, and I would immediately awake Karrington who would be sleep beside me and try to get over to Chaunce quickly. Sometimes, I remembered how he would end up on the floor or I would place him there to keep him from falling out of the bed. I would ease him down, because he would be shaking so terribly. He would usually be limp and lethargic after having a seizure and sometimes would just sleep for a while. I had times when I tried to pick him up to help him get back into bed, and as I would try to lift him from behind, I recalled pleading with him to help me to lift his body, but he just could not, and that's was when I decided to just place a pillow under his head, cover his body, and let him rest there until he could come around. Chaunce had gained an enormous amount of weight due mostly to his appetite coming from taking so many medicines. The majority of the time my husband would be out of town and not there when Chaunce had seizures, and it would just be me along to handle any medical problems that might come up. Karrington was not able to help much, but would do all she could.

Chaunce was a very sick child, but he still had the strength to torment and pick on his little sister. He continued to do this whenever he could. My strength was about to give out. Between caring for them and being a referee between him and Karrington I was drained of all my energy and strength. It had gotten to the point that it seemed like I was here and then I was not here. My husband, as much as he may have wanted to help, was simply unable to be there at critical times, due to his work schedule. I needed his support so much. I would sometimes find myself crying and just stressed almost to the end. I believe it to be true when I hear and read in the Bible that "God will not put any more on you than you can bear". I prayed to God to give me strength and bless us to see one more day. I could feel myself getting weaker, and weaker, and my heart was beginning to experience strange pains, I did not know if I was threatening a heart attack or stroke or what. When I tried to talk to my husband he did not seem to have even a clue as to the stress our family was going through. I love my children and always tried to let them know that. It did not matter how bad I felt, I knew that putting my children first was my main priority. For me, my children would always come first, that was something that I did not even have to think about, I guess as a mother, we just feel that way about our children from having motherly instincts. Even when my husband was not around, I knew that the Lord would be my strength, and he never let me down, NEVER!!!!

During the next few weeks, something sort of strange seemed to happen. Chaunce's behavior was beginning to change, but I did not really understand what was bringing it about, or pick up on it until a little later. I noticed that he seemed to hug me quite a bit, and give me a kiss on the jaw. He always was affectionate, but he seemed to be doing this much more than usual. I even caught him hugging Karrington. But, because of his past behavior, I immediately jumped to the conclusion that he was trying to hurt her or wrestle with her and it frightened me. When I asked Chaunce what was he doing?, he replied, I'm just giving my baby sister a hug. I caught him doing this several times during that week. But again, I did not think anything strange about that. I guess I was just so relieved that he was not trying to hurt her, and was finally being kind to her. I also remembered how I always told Chaunce to clean out his drawers of his chest. He loved to collect toys and all kinds of boy gadgets he had come across. Every time I would say to him, "Clean out those drawers or else I am going to empty them all out." Well, on one Sunday afternoon, September 24, 2006, I remembered my husband John had taken the children out to visit with his family members, and while they were gone, I decided to clean out Chaunce's chest drawers. I was upset when I went to put away some of his clothes that I was washed and found his chest drawers still in a mess. I got a couple of trash bags and picked out anything I thought was valuable to him and dumped everything else in the trash bags. When I was doing this I did not think of this as strange or unusual. However, as I think back on it now, I wonder if that was another sign of what was about to happen. Even, as I spoke to Chaunce's teacher, who was so wonderful and patient with him, she even mentioned to me that Chaunce gave her a big hug at school, and that even though all the students have their times for when they would give her a hug, Chaunce had wrapped his arms around her so tight and she could also tell that it felt different. There was something just different about his hug that day, she said. My son, Chaunce could not play many sports at all, due to his severe medical problems, such as the kidney transplant, the traumatic brain injury, the seizures, and all. He always felt sad though I know to have to sit on the sidelines, and watch the other boys play and run. He also had to wear a helmet for protection due to his severe and unpredictable seizures.

Many days Chaunce's teacher would take the class students to a nearby park to play ball, either football, kickball, soccer ball, etc., Sis. Daniels told me that Chaunce would sit close by and just watch the children running back and forth, back and forth, and she could see the pain in his face of having to always be left out of that. We discussed how much this seemed to hurt him and how much I wished he could be active in sports like all little boys long to do. She mentioned to me; however, on that one particular day, Thursday, September 28, 2006, as I was picking him up from school, that they all had been to the park, and that Chaunce did not seem to care about sitting on the side as the other students played ball. She told me that Chaunce had the time of his life. He threw that helmet off of his head, and took off running along side the other boys. He seemed to be so happy when he did this, and I know that this was something he wanted to do all of his life, JUST BE A LITTLE BOY, JUST TO BE A LITTLE BOY!!! His teacher said that she could tell that his heart was bursting over with so much joy. As she told this to me, I began to reflect and recall all the times when Chaunce would see other kids playing different contact sports, like football, baseball, soccer ball, and even karate, and he would ask me "Mom, can I play?" or "Why can't I play with them?" I would have to be the one to break his heart and say to him, you know it is because of your kidney transplant, or it is because of the seizures you have. I don't want you to get injured anymore. I even had to tell him one day that he may never be able to ride a motorcycle or bike, and this was devastating to him. I recalled a couple of years before, when Chaunce was about eight years old. We were at a local gas station getting gas, and before we left a group of young men rode up on some very nice motorcycles. There had to have been about 8-10 motorcycles. Chaunce always was one for starting a conversation. He told one of the motorcyclists that he really liked their motorcycles. The man replied, and told Chaunce that he would probably have one of his own someday. I looked over and told the young man that Chaunce had several medical problems, such as his seizures, brain injury and kidney transplant, and that because of that he would never be able to ride on a motorcycle. The young man could see how excited Chaunce was about the motorcycles, and said to Chaunce, "Would you like to try out my bike? He took Chaunce and placed him on the seat of his motorcycle, placed a helmet on Chaunce's head and turned on the engine. He allowed Chaunce to have an opportunity to receive one of the most exciting experiences of a lifetime. Even though Chaunce just sat on the motorcycle, this I knew was something he would never forget. I looked over at that young man, and he gave me nod. As we walked away, I told him THANK YOU!! And I could tell from his facial expression that he knew so much how I felt.

On Thursday, September 28, 2006, I remembered it being just a somewhat normal day. I was able to get the children to school that day and worked the day teaching my students. I had a doctor's appointment that afternoon and remembered having to get permission to leave early. I recalled having to run and get Karrington from school and then running to my appointment, being a little late. I felt so tired and drained, and my body was so tired. That morning I remembered I awoke with Chaunce having a seizure and recalled getting him through his seizure spell, which was a difficult seizure for him. When I ran late leaving the doctor's office, I called and asked the sitter to keep Chaunce a little longer after school, but that I was on my way to pick him up. There was a bad car accident with injury on my way, and that held me up even longer. I remembered getting Chaunce and going by my mother's house to complete his homework before we left for my choir rehearsal. His lessons were always centered on God, mainly because he attended a Christian school, which was something I was so thankful for, Chaunce learned and talked about God everyday. He truly enjoyed learning about him and all his wonderful works. He especially enjoyed when we read about how God created heaven and earth. We left for choir rehearsal and as soon as we got there, Chaunce saw one of the youth directors and ran up and gave her a big hug. I remembered she told him hello, and said to him that they had snacks in the youth house next door. He took off running over there and the children played on the church grounds that evening as we rehearsed. He and Karrington were having just a wonderful time playing outside with the other children.

After we left the church, I took Chaunce and Karrington by to eat dinner at a neighborhood restaurant, which we all enjoyed eating there every Thursday night and just whenever we could. I recall as we went through the serving line, Chaunce asked to get some broccoli and rice casserole. He loved that, and I told him he could have some of mine since he already had two vegetables on his plate. I was trying to cut back on his calories. We sat down and ate and I gave him my bowl. We talked as we normally did and that night Chaunce sat with us. Sometimes, he had gotten where he wanted to sit at a table beside us, I guess so he would seem more grown up. As we left, the children each got balloons, which I could never understand why, because they would either let them go up in the sky, even before we could hardly get outside, or they would just get burst, and I would hear a sound go pop, and one or the other of them would be screaming about it. I also recalled before getting into the truck, that Karrington's balloon was off floating into the sky, and Chaunce had his orange balloon in his hand, which he wanted to keep. For some reason, he did not want to get it blown up that time. We all had no idea that only hours from now, our lives would be changed forever, and never again be the same, as we had come to know it. I noticed as we walked to the truck, Chaunce seemed to walk slowly behind Karrington and myself, and he did not seem to be like the Chaunce we knew that would take off running and racing to the finish line. I even remembered how I commented on how much better behaved they both had become. I was able to go places with both of them not fussing or fighting and they would be patient with me as well, as they waited until I got my hair done or even my nails done. I had to come to realize at that point that my little children were growing up and they were not my little babies anymore. Even their attitudes had both changed for the better. After getting home, the kids got ready for bed, and sat on the ottoman in the living room watching T.V., while I prepared Chaunce's night medications. They sat there peacefully which was strange considering how something would always happen when I was not around when they watched the television, either fighting, fussing, kicking, or something. When I called Chaunce to get his medicine, he immediately came into the kitchen, which was something else odd to happen. I would so many times have to call him several times just to get him to come to take his medicines. When he came into the kitchen, he made a comment. He said, "see mom, I came to get my medicine like you called me, I did what you asked me." I told him yeah Chaunce, you did. I'm proud of you. I guess he said this because I remembered telling him one day that if he loved me like he often said he did, he would obey me when I called his name and do as I said. I also remembered that I was standing in the doorway in the kitchen and Chaunce came up to me and gave me a big tight hug. I knew it felt different, but I guess like many of us do, I didn't think anything special about it. Well, after that we all got in my bed to go to sleep, and I recalled asking

Chaunce to get up and turn down the light. He got right up and did as I asked of him. He was being my sweet little Chaunce. It seemed as if when we closed our eyes, it was as if a cloud came over us that just had us completely unconscious. I don't ever remember sleeping that sound. About 4:30 a.m. in the morning, my husband called as he normally did to check on us and to see how things were going. He did call somewhat earlier than he normally would have. I sat down on the side of the bed next to Chaunce. I told him that everything was fine and to go by Chaunce's school and pick him up to get a hair cut. I hung up the telephone and went around the bed to my side to lie back down. I noticed that Chaunce's arm was up over his head and very close to Karrington's face. I went to reach his arm to let it down, and it felt very strangely stiff. It scared me so much, so I got up and immediately ran around the bed to his side. I turned the light on and turned him over, and I began to SCREAM!! I remembered saying Chaunce No!! My Chaunce was gone. I could tell by his face and the color he had turned. He had passed away during the night, they said probably shortly after he had lied down. I guess when I turned him over it scared me so, I remembered letting his body go, and he just went back down on the pillow, his body had turned like a stiff board.

All I could say, was "Oh my God, Oh My God!!! I still to this day, have that image in my head. Karrington heard me yelling and screaming to get up, but I guess she thought he was having another seizure as he had had so many nights. I told her that Chaunce was gone; he left us during the night. I called 911 and was frantic and screaming so hysterically, but I was able to calm down to tell the dispatch person that my son was dead, and to send an ambulance. I then called my sister in law and brother in law still upset and crying uncontrollably. They could not understand what I was saying at first, but I was able to get out that Chaunce was not breathing and to come over right away. My brother in law, who was in Security at a local hospital immediately, came over. In fact, he made it there before the ambulance got there. He was able to calm me down some. He also went over to Chaunce and checked for a pulse, which he did not have one. He called back over to my sister in law, and told her what had happened. The next few hours seemed like I was having an awful nightmare, and I would soon wake up. It finally sank into my head that this was real. An angel had come during the night and taken my Chaunce home to see our God. Our Lord and Saviour, Jesus Christ. He was now with his loving Uncle Cleavon, who had preceded him in death. Chaunce missed him so much; he was a Godfather to him in every sense of the word. I thought to myself. He was probably the angel that came and took him away during the night. It was like God kept us asleep so that we would not change his plans for Chaunce or our lives. I did not remember turning over or moving, just being completely out. He was taken peacefully and quietly as we slept. I knew this was God's plan and we had no control over it, even though it hurt so much, so very much!!

The next few hours it seemed like I was standing in my body, but I was not really there physically. It seemed as if I was watching things happening, people going in and out of the house, family members, friends, neighbors, the coroner, sheriff's deputies, paramedics, etc., saying things, asking questions, and my body was there but my spirit was standing nearby watching these things happen. I just wanted to wake up from this terrible nightmare. The telephone rang, and it was my husband, he had made it back to town and was at his job. I had called his job earlier and told them to have him to call as soon as he returned from Texas. I just did not want him to go to Chaunce's school to pick him up and not see him there or find out the awful news from someone there. It started to remind me of when his mother had passed away the year before. I remembered having to tell him about that when he returned from his Dallas run. I couldn't believe it was happening again. There was something different this time though. We were all especially afraid for John and his reactions because only six (6) months earlier he had gone through a triple heart-bypass and was still recovering from that surgery. We were all worried about that and whether or not he had taken his heart medications before we told him about Chaunce. When he arrived at home, he probably knew something was wrong, especially seeing all the cars and emergency vehicles in the yard. He knew something had happened, but he just did not know what. When he entered the house, we sat John down on the bed and told him what had happened, and that Chaunce was gone. He broke down crying and just could not believe this was really happening. Only a few hours earlier I had just told him on the telephone that everything was fine, not realizing take my son out on a stretcher. I just broke down crying. I noticed that Chaunce had his hand folded up with something in it. When the funeral directors opened his hand, I saw it was the orange balloon Chaunce had gotten the night before while we were out to dinner. I had no idea that he was even still holding on to that balloon. I just began to think how much Chaunce loved going to that restaurant and getting a balloon. We did this almost every Thursday night. I just said to myself, my baby must have had that feeling of leaving us and just wanted to keep and hold on to something that brought him so much joy. Oh, my Chaunce, my Chaunce.

The next few days were spent making phone calls, planning Chaunce's funeral service, and trying to understand why he was taken away so soon from us, and at such a young age. We found ourselves breaking down, having quiet crying moments, but also remembering the good times we had shared with Chaunce, and all the wonderful memories we would keep in our hearts. Even though Chaunce had many issues with his behavior, mostly due to trauma he had to endure, we knew that our Chaunce was a sweet little boy, who just wanted to live his life as other little boys did, and just wanted to be accepted for who he was, medical problems and all. He did have such a loving heart, and a kind spirit. Even though our family dealt with so many struggles and tribulations, God had also placed a very special child in our lives and allowed us to share special memories, which we will always treasure, such as the family trip we had just taken that summer to Six Flags in Texas. My husband was always concerned about cost and budgeting, but I am so thankful that we had a chance to really enjoy time together as a family. This was something that never really occurred. But I know that this was an

Karrington were when they came back around.

The next few days were so unbearable. We got through only with the strength of the Lord, that I know for sure. I remember what it says in the bible about how God puts you through tests in order to sometimes test your faith and trust in him. And, that I believe, because if not for my faith and trust in him, I believe I would probably have gone away with Chaunce, just not being able to deal with my grieving and our loss. People all around us were so kind and supportive. They were truly a comfort to my entire family, as well as, myself. They made us realize how much they truly cared for us. They were there to offer us tremendous support, knowing that even though we had been through already so much, that was nothing like losing a child, especially so young. Karrington was having such a difficult time realizing and accepting the loss of her brother. Even though they would often fight and argue, and have sibling rivalries, Karrington knew that her brother Chaunce was gone and during the next several days on our way to school, and while driving through town, she would ask me questions that I just could not answer or even deal with, because every time I seemed to talk about Chaunce to anyone, I just could not help breaking down into tears. I would have to hold back my tears when she asked me questions like, "mom, can we go to the funeral home and bring Chaunce back with us? "How can Chaunce breathe under the ground when he is in that casket? I would always tell her that we would see him again one day, but she was just too young to understand what I meant. There were so many days that I just wanted to fall down and cry my heart out, but each time, she would see me get upset and I would be worried about the impact that would have on her. I remember when we had gone to a local restaurant where the kids and I would often eat dinner. In fact, we had eaten there the night before Chaunce had passed. She and Chaunce would run up to the door trying to beat one another, pushing the handicap button for the automatic door. As we approached the walkway of the restaurant, only days after Chaunce's death, Karrington ran up and hit the door button and looked back and said, "I beat you Chaunce." That just tore my heart up inside and I could have just broken down right there at the door screaming. I realized at that moment that Karrington really had not accepted his death. It was as if she was still looking for him to return home one day, on this earth. I often looked over at her as we were sometimes riding in the car, and caught her just staring into space, and I would say, "Karrington, what is wrong, what are you thinking about? She would reply, oh nothing, but I knew she was thinking about her big brother and how much she was missing him. I knew we had gone through so much together in our lifetime, together as a family, but Karrington and Chaunce had gotten to the point where they were playing together, and showing their love and affection for each other as brother and sister. I found myself often thanking God, for bringing my children through the pain and suffering they had endured. I told Karrington one day, before the funeral to go ahead and cry, let your tears fall, it's ok. Karrington said, but I did not get a chance to tell Chaunce goodbye, mom. But, I looked at her and said, "Karrington, remember the last week or so before he passed, how I caught him hugging you and saying nice things to you, like saying he was hugging you to show you how much he loved you. Well, that was his way of telling you goodbye then, we did not realize it or know it at the time, that what he was doing was telling you goodbye, and he would miss you, but it was his way, we just did not realize it. Chaunce probably felt his death, and I know that God knew it. I told her, "See how the Lord did not let you see him pass away, see how he took him away peacefully as we all slept, and we did not realize what had happened until the next morning. I felt in my heart that this was how he wanted Chaunce to leave us. We did not have a chance to tell him bye, but we must remember that Chaunce will always be with us, in his spirit, he is always around us, he is our little angel.

The next few days, I prayed to God to give us the strength to make it through. I often found myself saying, Lord, I know you are right there for us, helping to hold us up, and I have faith that you will not leave us in our time of sorrow, but God it is so hard, so hard to make it through. Every time that I would speak to someone about Chaunce, somebody would come up to me and tell me of the impact Chaunce had on their lives, I would become so full, and my throat would be filled with a lump so big I could not swallow. I realized then that so many people in our lives knew how special a person Chaunce was. Even though he had some episodes of bad behaviors, mostly I think it was due to his brain injury, and his negative experiences with children not understanding his disability, Chaunce did indeed, have a big heart. He was there for us when we felt down. I recalled one day my husband was reflecting on Chaunce, and he said he remembered the night he was in the bed with Chaunce, sitting there talking, and Chaunce could see that his dad was feeling down and deep in thought. Well, Chaunce asked, "dad what's wrong?", and his dad said, oh, nothing, I'm just thinking about Grandma Almedia and Bill, they were my husband's mother and brother whom had recently passed on. Chaunce told him "dad, you'll get a chance to see them one day, don't cry. My husband just said, yeah, you're right. My husband said, he told Chaunce, that he loved him, and that I loved him. Chaunce replied, "dad, why do you all love me so much? Chaunce's dad said, well, just because you're so special, special to all of us. He said, Chaunce just laughed and smiled and went off to sleep.

During the next day or so while planning Chaunce's home going, we came across many pictures of him from when he was a little boy up until his last weeks before his death. And as I reflected on Chaunce's life and these pictures, there was always something so obvious, even though Chaunce had always been a very sick child, struggling over one medical hurdle after another, it never showed on his face, whether in person or on pictures, he always seemed to be to everyone, just a happy go lucky little boy. The Lord had revealed to me how Chaunce's life impacted so many lives of his friends, classmates, relatives, neighbors, and yes, even total strangers. I found myself crying often, and I just could not seem to hold back the tears. Thinking of all the things our family, especially Chaunce and I, had gone through, I thought "Lord, I would go through all of that again, if I could just have our son back," we were missing him so much!!!

The school Chaunce attended had called and as we planned his to present to us from the students at his school because they were missing him so much and wanted to show their love for him. Even though it was so painful going through old photos and memories of Chaunce, I was able to gather enough pictures to create the slide presentation. The next day, which was Wednesday or Thursday I believe, I could not seem to remember. My mind was as if I was in a dream and soon going to wake up and this was going to be just an awful nightmare. But then, reality set in and I realized that our Chaunce was indeed gone. I took his clothes to the funeral home and showed them a picture of how I wanted his hair to be cut. When time came to view his body before the public visitation, I sat there in the hallway of the funeral home with my husband and other family members waiting to go in, and I could feel my body so nervous, I felt so limp, almost like a bowl of jelly.

My husband was also taking it hard. This would be the first time he would be seeing Chaunce since he left going to work that night before he passed. He commented that he did not realize that when Chaunce gave him a hug goodbye he did not realize that it would be the last time he would see him alive. Well, we went in to see him, and our son looked so peaceful and had just a very calm, and restful look on his face. I realized at that point that our baby was now out of all of the pain and suffering he had endured all of his life, and was finally able to do things he could never do down here on earth. He could run, play ball, ride around on a bike, and just enjoy his life as a little boy should. I thought to myself that he was no longer in pain from awful seizures, and having to endure all those terrible needles, often one after another. Our son was now free, and resting in a most wonderful place. He was able now to be with his Godfather and

Uncle Clevon, whom he had missed so dearly, since his death only a few months earlier, as well as, other family members, close and dear to him. Our oldest daughter, Tiffani, had the most difficult time dealing with seeing him lying there. I felt it was probably because she and Chaunce had experienced the most difficult relationship, her trying to be the firm, oldest big sister, trying to make him mind and obey her, and Chaunce being the way he was, always fighting against her authority, despite my attempt to get her to understand that Chaunce, because of his brain injury, many times was not in his right mind, he did not realize often times even what he was saying or doing. And because of his brain injury, which the doctors had said, did affect his emotions, he really just could not help what he did or said. I know that Tiffani did love her brother and only wanted what was best for him. I could sense that Tiffani was having regrets of moments she and Chaunce had aired their differences, and she said something to me that just put a lump in my throat. She told me that as she was in our living room writing her tribute to Chaunce, she felt something warm touch the side of her leg and it just stayed there for a moment. I told her that it was Chaunce coming to sit beside her to let her know that he had forgiven her for the bad times they had shared and just wanted her to know that he did also love her very much. I believe that unlike myself and my husband, Tiffani did not realize all the pain that Chaunce was enduring and had endured for the most part of his life, all the stares, and cruel comments made by other children, the way children picked on him because of his vulnerability or else his size. He had so much hurt in him from children treating him mean just because he acted different or looked different. They did not realize just how special a person he truly was. I remembered one day when Chaunce came up to me and said, "mom, I just wish I did not have to be sick all the time." I let him know that the Lord was there for him, even when others are not, and even one day if mom and dad are not here for you, just remember that the Lord is always right there by your side, and that you're one of his special angels sent down here on earth for a very special reason.

I think of all the pain so many parents with disabled children go through and how it must hurt them to have their child say that, knowing that many times there is nothing we can do as a parent, despite all the research and technology that has gone into finding cures for so many diseases and illnesses. But, you know, we can always PRAY and just place it in the Lord's hand. Just remember that he is the cure of all those illnesses. JUST PRAY!! JUST PRAY!!! JUST PRAY!!! CONTINUALLY!! WITHOUT CEASING!!! I can say for myself and for those parents of these precious children, that we must realize that God is in control and he has a plan for our children, just as he had a plan for our Chaunce, and remember that these are God's little angels sent here on earth to do God's will, whether it is to touch someone's life or make a difference in how we live and treat others. I reminded myself that even though Chaunce had gone through so much medically, God was always there to provide us with the resources we needed to take care of him, and to give us the strength when he knew we could not carry on any further. GOD WAS THERE!! GOD IS ALWAYS THERE!!! AND HE ESPECIALLY LOVES HIS LITTLE ANGELS!!!

During the family hour there were tributes made by Chaunce's friends and classmates, our friends, and close family members. As we did, they reflected on not just the sickness and pain Chaunce endured but also how they will have so many wonderful memories to keep of him of all the good times they had shared. There were songs and praise dances and his teacher presented the most heart filled poem she had written in memory of Chaunce. It was a poem of how she knew Chaunce felt. It was so wonderful and everyone in the chapel had tears in their eyes. The poem was entitled "HALLELUJAH I'M FREE", In loving memory of John C. Davis, II, written by his teacher, Sis. Joann Daniels:


HALLELUJAH I'M FREE!!!

I'm free to run, skip and play all day! Couldn't do it before because of my mental and physical delay.

I'm free to laugh, dance, and praise Hallelujah, I'm free is what I'll forever say!

I'm exceedingly grateful to have been born, so when you remember me, please don't mourn.

My life on earth was short I know, not enough time to live and to grow, but the merciful savior delivered me from all distress, gave me a new mind, a new body, and an everlasting rest.

A new name I've received, a new home to abode. New friends I have now acquired, but I shall never forget the old.

Hallelujah, I'm free......I'm Free........I'm Free!!!!!

I'm free to love, hope, and to forgive. Thank God Jesus Christ, He died so I can eternally live.

Chaunce's teacher was showing so much expression. As the poem was being read so beautifully and eloquently, I could not help but think about the day we went to pick out a cemetery plot, and a little bird was walking around right there in that same area, and I just know it was Chaunce's little spirit letting me know that he was ready to be laid to rest right there. There was a change or two in the placement of the plot, and it was so amazing how at the end, the plot we chose was exactly where that little bird was hopping around. There I knew was where he would be laid to rest. It was under a huge oak tree which had a chime making such a wonderful and peaceful sound as the wind blew. I also thought to myself how yes, he was now FREE, especially after my sister had told me that she had a vision of Chaunce a day or so before the family hour and funeral, and it was one of Chaunce having such fun just running around "Jordan's River." My sister told me that the Lord showed her that Chaunce was just fine and at peace.

As the family hour came to an end our pastor made remarks, and mentioned that little John (Chaunce), had so many people who loved him. He made mention that in the slide presentation, all the pictures showed him with people around him, either family or friends, and that this showed how much he was loved. I turned around to look back in the room and was so amazed at how many people were at the family hour. There was no more room to sit and people were in the foyer standing. I just could not hold back my tears, because I knew and realized how much they cared for Chaunce, and our family. It was just so overwhelming. Afterwards, everyone just came up and gave us hugs and words of encouragement, and letting us know how much they cared. The Lord was truly in that place because he was giving my husband and I the strength we needed to make it through.

I recalled how a little boy John had met in kindergarten, had so much courage to get up in front of everyone that night and acknowledge how much Chaunce meant to him and how much he was going to miss him. I remembered the day John "Chaunce" came home talking about this little boy who kept picking on him and was taking his toys. I was just amazed to see this little boy a few weeks later and he was just about half of Chaunce's size. I thought it was some large, tall child maybe twice my baby's size. They remained best friends up until John's death, and his little speech had touched our hearts so much, that I could not hold back my tears.

The next day was the day of our son's funeral. As we prepared to load the funeral cars and during our drive to town, I could still see the feeling of disbelief on my husband's face. I knew he felt as I did that this could not be happening, but we realized that in fact, our son Chaunce was gone. As we were escorted into church behind the casket I could not help but think of how happy we were when we were finally given a son, and knowing that when we entered our home again, our lives would never be the same, and how we would now have a wonderful baby boy to bring home, despite all the odds that were against him, and all the comments of hopelessness that were given to us about our baby's chance for survival. It was so ironic how I now had the feeling of going home after the funeral services and knowing that when we entered our home again, our lives would once more be changed forever, only this time we would have a loss of our son, and the feeling this time was not one of joy and happiness, but one of pain and extreme sadness. I just don't know if there is a more painful feeling than one of a parent suffering the loss of their child. The funeral service was filled with songs, praise, and tribute of caring and loving memories, as well as, support. The pastor mentioned again during his eulogy, how Chaunce had touched the lives of so many, how he always greeted you with a big hug, and smile. The church was filled with loved ones who had traveled far and near, many of Chaunce's teachers, church members, co-workers, friends and family, and people who wanted to show us their love and support. Later, we returned home for the Re Pass and I just could not eat much of anything. Everyone was showing their concern and wanted to make sure that I put some food in my stomach, but I just had no appetite. I looked over at my husband and knew that even though he too was trying to be strong as he visited with relatives and friends, I could tell that he was hurting and filled with pain and so much sadness. But I happened to look over at the side of the yard where there was a little slope on the edge of the grounds near a flowerbed. I saw a little kitten that I had never seen before, peeping out from behind some of the shrubs and I just know that was God letting me know that it was Chaunce's little spirit. Yes, his little spirit was in that precious kitten there, and he was able to see how much he was dearly loved and so truly missed by everyone.

During Chaunce's Re Pass, we received a telephone call of more awful news. We were told that my husband's sister, who lived in a nearby town and had been suffering from a terminal illness, had lost her fight. Everyone was not sure about telling my husband with having so much already to deal with, but later, we decided to tell him. So, just the next weekend, we were there at her funeral offering her family support. My pastor commented the next week in bible class that Sister Rita was a very strong lady. I guess referring to the fact that shortly after having a funeral service for our son Chaunce, we were in attendance at another family member's funeral, and consoling them. It was hard to understand I guess for some, how we were able to endure so much tragedy. Well, my thoughts were that it wasn't me, but it was the Lord, holding both my husband and myself up. HE IS THE ONE TO GIVE YOU STRENGTH. HE IS THERE HOLDING US UP WHEN OUR EARTHLY BODY NO LONGER CAN. HE IS THE ONE WHO IS KEEPING US IN OUR RIGHT MIND WHEN OUR WORLD IS BEING TORN APART BEFORE OUR EYES!!!!

Well, it is almost one year and eight months since my son Chaunce's death. Life will never be the same, and not one day goes by without us thinking of Chaunce and wishing he was here again with us. People always pass me and ask how am I doing? All I can say is I am taking one day at a time, and yes God is giving us the strength to hold on. Every day, I live life grateful to see another day, I have a smile on my face, I act cheerful, and hold back my tears many times. But you know what, all I want to do sometimes is cry, scream and yell out so, so, loud!!! I guess I am waiting for that day when I can no longer hold my sadness in, I miss my Chaunce so much!! Lord God, I miss him so much!! That day is coming I know, when I am going to just fall down on the floor, and yell, scream, and grieve for my Chaunce like I am doing on the inside. I don't know when it will happen, I don't know where it will happen, but I feel like it will be soon, very soon.

I can tell any parent to love your children, love them unconditionally. No matter what they may do in life, love them. If you have a child with a mental illness or sickness, love them even more. I wished so many times that I had spent more quality time with my Chaunce. But, I realize that as a parent, often times we don't realize how important it is just to sit and talk, not about chores, not even about school, but just talk about life, talk about them. Enjoy your children!!! Enjoy your children!!! Treat every moment as if it is your last time together. I think back now on times that we wasted fussing about small things that should not even matter. Sometimes, when our children are acting up or behaving in awful ways, it is not because they are bad or because they don't love us. It may be simply because they are hurting and just don't know how else to show their feelings and cry for help and understanding. They need us as parents, they need our love, our support, and understanding. When a special needs child, such as Chaunce, is treated so mean by other children and picked on or called names because of their illness, because of their size, or because they don't think like other children, it really hurts them. We should teach all children that God made all angels. Children who are going through serious medical problems or live their lives with chronic diseases should be given a chance to enjoy life as any other child should.

Recently, I was in a restaurant sitting waiting for a take out order and this parent came in with her child. It was a little boy, who was about Chaunce's size and age. He even had his hair cut similar to Chaunce's. I could tell within a matter of minutes that he was possibly a special needs child. Even though he looked perfectly healthy, like Chaunce, I guess I could tell by some of the things he was doing. He also seemed to be hyperactive. The other parent came in shortly after. This child just reminded me so much of Chaunce. I noticed that he was making spit bubbles, and how the hostess at the restaurant was looking at him. All I could think of was that I wanted to tell his parents to love him, I don't care if he can't sit still or say or does things that may be inappropriate, LOVE HIM. Show him that love every day. Tell him that everyday. Most of all, be there for him, and spend quality time with him. Remember that he is a gift from God. I wanted to say this to those parents so badly, but I did not know how they would react. I guess they were probably wondering why I was starring at them so.

I also realized and learned from this life experience, that we were not being as God wanted us to be, which was humble. My husband and I were blessed from the beginning of our marriage, even before Chaunce was born. Even to the point of sometimes becoming boastful. I did not realize at that time how disappointing this was to our Lord God. I look back now on our lives and I know now for myself, that many of the trials, tribulations, and suffering we went through was, in fact, for a reason, it happened for a reason. We must remember that everything that happens in our life is for a REASON!! One of which was to help us realize who exactly is in control of our lives. We understand that life is not about materials things or what you have or can accomplish, but is and should be about pleasing GOD!! I think about how we both loved Chaunce so much, and many times because of the stress we faced, it was taking a toll on our marriage. Chaunce was able to make us stronger as parents, he made us stronger as a family, and he helped us to make our marriage stronger. I just try to do all I can for others, realizing that it is not about us, it is about GOD!! Using what he has blessed us with to bless others. I'll tell anyone that material things and money are not about nothing. If you don't have the right heart, and a loving spirit, you don't have anything. All the money in the world can't buy you happiness, and it can't buy you good health. My husband, as well as, myself, seem to have a true understanding more now than ever, about what life is. Having our Chaunce and going through what we went through for the past ten or eleven years with him, has taught us so much. God has created in us a new heart, a new spirit. It has taught us to be patient, and to wait on the Lord. I truly realize that nothing is possible without having God on your side.

One day, as some of my family members and I sat and talked, I mentioned that I had spoken to someone, a lady at a salon, and as I was telling her about the book and Chaunce, and testifying about God's goodness, she mentioned something to me that almost knocked me over. She was talking about when people nearly die, they sometimes pass over to the other side and they have gotten a glimpse at how wonderful and beautiful heaven is and what is there waiting for them. However, if they do not stay and return to the land of the living, they are staying against their will, and sometimes feeling resentful. I was told about how the love of their family and friends keep them hear on this side, even though they are fighting against us. I thought about how Chaunce nearly died when he almost drowned in the bathtub on the night of Sept. 13, 2001, and how he had turned so pale and his lips were purple. I kept trying CPR to get him to breathe. He too, had probably crossed over for that short period of time and got a chance to see inside heaven and experience that wonderful sense of peace. That I feel, might explain why all these years since his near drowning, he acted so different. To me he acted as if he was trying to get me upset and angry with him. Many days I kept wondering what am I doing wrong to cause him to act so negative and mean towards me, when all I was trying to do was to love him and care for him, making sure his medical needs were met. My love for Chaunce was so strong, and it was an unconditional love that we all should have for our children. He knew I loved him in spite of what trials we went through.

As my family and I continued to talk, I began to break down in tears, because what I had come to realize was also giving me a sense of peace and understanding. I miss Chaunce so much, in fact, the entire family does not go by a day without thinking about him, and the wonderful times we shared while he was here on earth. However, as my sister said to me, "Chaunce was here for a purpose, he touched so many lives during the short time he was here on earth. He had fulfilled God's plan for him, and God called him home to rest. She was stating that God had chosen me as Chaunce's mom, because he would be able to use my body, soul and spirit to care for Chaunce. God knew it would be overwhelming for many to endure, but he trusted me to care for this angel while he was here on earth doing God's will. God supplied all that I needed in order to take care of our Chaunce. I can imagine Chaunce when he entered the gates of heaven and God telling him well done true and faithful servant, well done!!!!

84

A TESTIMONY TO THOSE PARENTS WHO MIGHT BE ON THE VERGE OF GIVING UP. JUST REMEMBER TO KEEP THE FAITH AND PLACE THESE WORDS OF ENCOURAGEMENT IN YOUR HEART. BUT WHATEVER YOU DO, DON'T GIVE UP, DON'T GIVE UP!!!!!

From all the trials and tribulations I've been through, I have learned how to lean on God. God is my Rock. Don't quit, don't give up. God was helping me to develop my faith. I walked through the valley of the shadow of death. I remembered reading this scripture all my life and never until my experience, did I truly realize exactly what it meant. Through all my struggles, pain, and misery, I made it out, and I am still standing. Understanding what faith means, I was being tested and tried, going through trials from within to help determine my patience with the Lord. I realized now that things don't happen when I am ready for them to happen, but when God is ready for me to receive them. In the mist of my struggles, I just knew it was my Lord God who was bringing us through the fire and through the flood. It was like going through fire, but not getting burned. GOD made it so we did not get burned. Lord Jesus all along was testing my faith, times when I felt like giving up, and feeling that I had no one to care or talk to, I came through the struggles, through the flames, out of the valley and made it through the storms. And yes, I am still standing praising my GOD!! I still have praise, I have a testimony, and though all I have been through, I still have that wonderful joy within. Through so much of my life I felt as if we endured one turmoil after another, many times looking at my family, as well as, myself as dysfunctional. I did not realize at that time that God was ordering our steps. In fact he was leading our way. So many of us today, just don't realize who is in control. GOD IS IN CONTROL!!! GOD IS IN CONTROL!!! I began working on my relationship with God, talking with him often. I shared my thoughts and my pain, and he knew what I was going through. I know now that he will always be there to fight your battles and carry you through. When I finally came to realize this, I had this overwhelming sense of peace. And as the bible says, "He is the prince of peace."

Lord, how true that is.

I have come to realize that when trouble is all around you, coming at you from all angles, and you are suffering trials and tribulations in your life, it is not happening to bring you down. God is putting you through those things to help bring you up, and make you stronger. Even sometimes when it seems that there are so many afflictions upon the righteous, know for yourself that God will bring you out of each and every one of them. DON'T GIVE UP!!! DON'T GIVE UP!!! KEEP THE FAITH IN THE LORD!!! And most importantly, have that unconditional love for your children, as God has for us. We must always remember that our children are in deed a gift from God.

God uses us for his glory and he wants us to go out into the world and tell others of his marvelous work, and tell others of his goodness and mercy. Whenever I think back about all the trials and suffering my family, especially Chaunce went through, I realize now that it was all for a reason. Chaunce's suffering was not in vain. God had Chaunce here for a purpose. He was God's angel sent here on earth to do God's will. And I know now that I must go out and tell the world just how good God is, you all just don't know. It makes me feel like fire shut up in my bones. I have just got to tell somebody. When my family members passed, it rained. All of the suffering Chaunce endured each time, it rained, and Lord, when the death of Chaunce came, it rained, the Lord opened the flood gates of heaven.

I think back on times I just wished I had demonstrated more patience with my children, in particularly, Chaunce. I remembered one night when I got home from town and we had all eaten, Karrington, Chaunce and myself. I had brought my husband a dinner home for him. Even though Chaunce should not have been hungry, he had a tendency to ask his dad for food from his plate. I would plead with my husband not to give him any more food, and let him know that he had already had enough to eat. Despite my plea, my husband would give Chaunce more food anyway. Well, this particular night Chaunce went to bed, and over in the night, I noticed that Chaunce was coughing quite a bit. I sat him up a few times to clear his throat. After my husband left about 2:00 a.m. for work we went back to bed. Chaunce was lying next to me and I guess within a matter of minutes, Chaunce threw up (vomited) everywhere, and because he was lying on his back, it went straight up in the air landing all over his chest, on his face, on my face, and in my hair. It was just a complete mess. I was so upset because I knew it was mainly because Chaunce had overeaten. Something I was really trying to avoid. And my husband I felt was the blame for this and of course he was gone now and nowhere to help in the clean up. I guess I tried my best not to lose my temper or get upset, but this was something I knew did not have to happen. As I think back on that night, I wished I had more patience and had just made light of what had happened. However, Chaunce could tell that I was upset. Karrington was asleep in the baby bed, and I was spending the next hour or so trying to clean up the mess, with only two more hours before I had to get up and start my day, getting everybody ready.

Life is so short, and we should realize that every precious moment we waste being upset or angry about something our children may do, are precious moments we can never get back. This reminds me so much of Chaunce and myself and how I wished I had not been so serious so much of the time and how I should have really just made light of little things that should not have even mattered.

The last couple of years I have definitely begun to take things as they are. I have made a promise to myself to live life one day at a time, and to stop and smell the roses. Don't worry about things I can't change or don't have control over. Remembering that if we are to inherit God's blessings, we must accept and learn to endure the storms and rain he places in our lives, as well as, the sunshine. Spending more quality time now with my family is more important than anything, and just remember to always give GOD all the praise!! PRAISE THE LORD!!

# Acknowledgements

Asleen Brown, My wonderful mother
Tiffani C. Brown
Karrington Davis
Sis. JoAnn Daniels
My family members
Mrs. Maria Berry
Mrs. Charlotte Graham
Mr. Cleavon Matthews
Dr. Melinda Ray
The Faculty and Staff of University of Mississippi Medical Center –
    Nephrology Department
The Faculty and Staff of LeBonheur's Children Hospital –
    Nephrology Clinics
Pastor Randy LeFlore, and the Friendship M.B. Church Family
Mrs. Ruby Shaffer
Mrs. Vanessa Edmonds

Printed in the United States
146217LV00002B/35/P